Issues
A Guide to Heart Health

A distinctively Christian Perspective

By
Dr. Bob & Laura Nichols

Copyright © 2007 by Dr. Bob & Laura Nichols

Issues
A Guide to Heart Health
A distinctively Christian Perspective
by Dr. Bob & Laura Nichols

Printed in the United States of America

ISBN 978-1-60477-040-7

All rights reserved solely by the author. The author guarantees all contents are original and do not infringe upon the legal rights of any other person or work. No part of this book may be reproduced in any form without the permission of the author. The views expressed in this book are not necessarily those of the publisher.

Unless otherwise indicated, Bible quotations are taken from the New American Standard Version. Copyright © 1999 by The Zondervan Corporation.

www.xulonpress.com

Table of Contents

Introduction xiii

Preparing for Surgery

Chapter One - Asking the Tough Question 17
    Did the devil make me do it?

Chapter Two - Starting Over 25
    Do I really have to be born-again?

Diagnosing the Problem

Chapter Three – Soul Mapping 31
Understanding the Process: From Desires to Choices to Behavior

Chapter Four - Did my daddy make me do it? 43
    Unwrapping Trans-generational Behavior

Chapter Five – Soul Mapping II 49
    Understanding the Enemy's Strategies

Chapter Six – Our Ten Core Needs 63
Need Driven Behavior and the Ten Basic Needs of Every Person

Issues

Laying out the Tools

Chapter Seven - Here Come the Judge! 91
    How Judgments Perpetuate Undesired Behavior

Chapter Eight – What You Speak is what you Get 113
    Understanding Your Verbal Communication has Consequences

Chapter Nine - Vows & Inner Determinations. 121
    Understanding Negative Inward Determinations & Resolves

Chapter Ten – Offended!...107
    Understand the Nature of an Offence

Chapter Eleven – How to Say No!....................................125
    Understanding Boundaries & How to set them

Chapter Twelve - Wounds 131
    Different Types of Wounds & their Healing

Chapter Thirteen – Defilement, Soul Ties & Heart Writing.......149
    "Déjà vu," "Defilement" and "Heart Writing"

Chapter Fourteen – Lost Places of Your Soul 163
    When traumas delete your memory

Chapter Fifteen – The Children's Counseling Session 201
    Practical Guide to Counseling Procedures for Children

Chapter Sixteen – Understanding the Model 179
    Understanding "Christ-O-Therapy"

Appendix

Counseling Aid Sheet..201
Integrated Terms
Pre-Counseling Inventory 206
Christ-O-Therapy...204

Issues

Counseling Ledger 208
Child Information Form 209
Release of Liability 215
Release of Liability 215

Part II – Need Oriented Behavior

Chapter Seventeen – Introduction to Need Oriented Behavior
    Introduction to the History of Need Oriented Behavior

Chapter Eighteen – Core Need One – Need for Identity
    To Feel "Special, Valuable and A Feeling of Belonging

Chapter Nineteen – Core Need Two – Need for Reality to Feel "In-touch"
    Discussion of the Many Facets of Reality-detachment

Chapter Twenty – Core Need Three – Need to Feel Free to Make Decisions
    Discussion of Co-dependency and its Effects

Chapter Twenty-One – Core Need Four – Need to Trust
    To Feel I Can Trust Again - How to Reconnect Broken Trust

Chapter Twenty-Two – Core Need Five – Need for Responsibility & Accountability
    The Balance of Responsibility & Accountability

Chapter Twenty-Three – Core Need Six – The Need to Feel Loved & to Give Love
    What happens when the Need to Give & Receive Love is not fulfilled

Chapter Twenty-Four – Core Need Seven – The Need to Feel Preferred
    Infidelity Violates the Need to be Preferred

Chapter Twenty-Five – Core Need Eight – The Need to Feel Secure
Provision, Protection and Emotional Security

Chapter Twenty-Six – Core Need Nine – The Need for Integrity and Credibility
Single-minded and Single-heart, holding to a Moral Value System

Chapter Twenty-Seven – Core Need Ten – The Need to Feel Content

From Purpose to Passion to Joy to Contentment... How to Find Contentment

Conclusion

Acknowledgments

I wish to thank the many men and women of Redeemed Christian Fellowship who worked in the counseling ministry... working out the many practical tools that are taught in this book. I wish particularly to acknowledge Mike & Cindy Morgan who gave great leadership and insight especially to the section on Core Needs.

Special thanks go to my wife, Laura Nichols, who worked patiently with me encouraging the development of these training materials. Many of the ideas in this manual are hers, and in many ways, this manual is a joint effort.

Special thanks to my daughter Rebekah Nichols whose creative writing skills developed the story of Chapter four, "Did My Daddy Make Me Do It?"

Dedication

*T*his book is dedicated to my family who are absolutely fantastic! Through thick and thin they have always stood firm... believing and trusting and loving.

Laura... my wife
Our three children and their families
Rebekah Nichols ... and Stone
Jeremy & Rachael James... Skyleigh, Landon, and Canyon
Benjamin & Romay Nichols... and Eligh

And to my parents, Paul & Nell Nichols, to whom I am forever grateful for their love and support.

Introduction

Since the beginning of time, man has struggled with the *Issues of the Heart*. From his relationship with God, to his relationships with others, mankind has crippled his success, and detoured his destiny because of *Issues*. From addictions to obsessions, from habits to dysfunctions, we struggle…band aiding the symptom, unable to arrest the problem.

Times are changing. Five keys will consume counselors in the coming years. Consider the five consequences of the coming years.

1. Bioethics, and especially the *aging population* that is experiencing physical and mental infirmities, will be increasingly important.
2. People will struggle with the age-old issue of *pain and God's goodness*.
3. The widening gap between the *affluent and poor* will draw attention. Issues of poverty and subsequent inequalities will take focus.
4. *Marriages* will be overstressed. Divorce, remarriage, cohabitation and single parenting will increase.
5. Both religious tensions and urban crowding will increase conflict and stress. Hate, bitterness, and unforgiveness will characterize many people's daily lives. *Forgiveness* and *reconciliation* will become one of the major topics in Christian counseling.

[Taken from an article, "Five Mega-Trends Affecting Christian Counseling" by Dr. Everett L. Worthington, Jr., Ph.D.]

I recently had a man contact me that was struggling with an *issue*. He proceeded to tell me how his wife had left him and that when I heard her side of the story I would probably think that he was the worst husband and father in the world. When he finally paused to take a breath, I said to him, "John, do you want help, or do you simply want me to be your friend? Because if you want help, it will begin with your honesty and your willingness to be transparent. As long as you insist on projecting your desired persona to me, all I can be is your friend, unable to help. So which will it be…friend or counselor?" After a moment of silence, to my delight, he said, "counselor."

I then shared with John four things to do prior to our first meeting… things which would help us get to the root of the *issues*. These same four things will aid you in preparation for your own *open-heart surgery…*

1. *Don't pretend the problem isn't there.* An honest inventory is the place we will begin. Here are some questions to answer to aid you in your inventory. (See Pre-Counseling Worksheet in the appendix – iv, v, vi)

    - Describe who you are.
    - How do you deal with stress & pressure? (Workout, eat, movies, sports, read, etc.)
    - What is necessary in a relationship for you to trust the other person?
    - How do you show love to others?
    - Do you feel secure? What comprises this security?
    - Whom do you get affirmation from the most? Who do you desire affirmation from the most?
    - Describe you relationship to your father, listing the three most significant moments with him that have affected your life.

- Describe your relationship to your mother, listing the three most significant moments with her that affected your life.
- What is the worst offence you have experienced? How did you handle it?
- What makes you angry? How do you handle the situation when you get angry?
- When do you get most embarrassed? Describe the circumstances.
- When do you have the most trouble making decisions? Describe the circumstances.
- Describe the circumstances that cause you to feel the most rejected.
- When do you feel most content?

We must face the problem, but we must not become overwhelmed by the problem. The next step helps us face the problem and still keep it in perspective.

2. Take a *God Look*. It is one thing to feel, it is another to see. Most *issues* are activated by feelings…i.e. we "feel" angry, or we "feel" ashamed. A helpful step is to *see* what God sees concerning the areas with which we are struggling. Use the index at the back and read the verses concerning the *issue*s at hand.
3. *Ask for help*. In the midst of analyzing, remember that ultimately it is God who unravels the complexities of our *issues*. Ask God for help. In whatever way you connect with God, ask Him. In addition, as you pray, find a trusted friend or counselor who can be a sounding board and support for you. Remember that *issues of the heart* not only involve your relationship with God, but also your relationship with others.
4. *Begin to journal*. Ask yourself, what was the most important situation or feeling of this day? How did I handle it? How did it make me feel? Write these feelings down in your personal journal. This is an important part of "processing" the feelings within.

Did the devil make me do it?

Diagnostic Questions – Are there uncontrollable behavior patterns? Are these same destructive behavior patterns found in the parents? Are there "addictions" involved (drug, sexual, food, etc.)? Has there been a background (themselves or family) of occult involvement? Are there other "metaphysical" evidences (ESP, physic ability, out of body experiences, etc.)?
Prognosis – We will attempt to answer one of theology's most difficult questions: Can a Christian have a demon?
Remedy - As the roots & schemes are discovered, and the hearts wounds are healed, deliverance will take place.

It was several years ago that a friend of mine was in his college class listening to a guess speaker. The class was Psychology 101 at Concordia Lutheran College in Austin Texas, and the guest was a psychiatrist from a well-known *Christian* psychiatric firm. Given opportunity for questions, my friend asked the well-known psychiatrist, "Do you believe in demons? Are there really such things as demons and do they affect our lives? The doctor proceeded with this story.

"Until a few weeks ago I would have answered this question with a great hesitation. However, a few weeks ago I had a very unusual experience that answered many questions I had concerning this very subject. I have a client that I had been working with for over two years. I had documented some twenty-seven personalities within this woman. She was a classic "Multiple Personality" ("MP"). I called a friend of mine who had a Christian Counseling Center in the city. I knew of their reputation and success in dealing with "MP's" so I called and made an appointment for my client. The arrangement allowed me to sit in on the counseling session. When the day arrived, I met my client in the lobby of the Counseling Center, and we proceeded in.

We were met by a kind receptionist who introduced us to our counselors... who just happened to be two housewives with no professional training in psychology or psychiatry. What I watched unfold over the next two hours has forever changed my views on the subject of "demons." In a systematic way, these untrained housewives unraveled the layers of my client's *issues,* and then proceed to remove the false personalities until there was only one personality left."

For years, I kept connections with this wonderful psychiatrist. Years later he shared with me that he continued to see the lady for some two more years. In addition, as of her last appointment, this woman was still in her "right mind" with only one personality.

So the real question is, "Can a Christian have a demon?" In the first church I pastored, I was told by one of my church members who was a treasury agent; we learn to detect the counterfeit by sitting in a room for hours handling and inspecting real dollar bills. Then without our knowing, our instructor would slip in a counterfeit to see if we could detect it. We had to stay in the room until we were able to detect it. From this incredible lesson, I learned an important spiritual truth. If you know the *real thing*, you will have no trouble spotting a *counterfeit.*

First, it is important to understand that people can be affected by demons. It is hard to define and differentiate the degree to which a person is hindered by demonic influence. People can argue about whether someone is harassed, possessed, or influenced, but there is no question that demons exist and that they affect people. The Bible has many stories of Jesus and the disciples casting out demons.

When we speak of demons, we need to make our notes from the most authoritative of all sources, the Bible. So let's do a bit of Bible Study.

Bible Study

The Bible seems to indicate that people outside a vital real connection with God are subject to demonic influence.

- Ephesians 2:1-3 *".... in which you once walked according to the course of this world, according to the prince of the power of the air, the spirit who now works in the sons of disobedience, among whom also we all once conducted ourselves in the lusts of our flesh..."* This scripture shows that those outside this vital connection with God are influenced by demons.
- Colossians 1:13 *"He has delivered us from the power of darkness and translated us into the kingdom of the Son of His love."*

So, the Bible seems to indicate that those outside "vital real connection" with God are influenced by the demons. Yet the real question is can a Christian, one with a vital real connection with God, be influenced by a demon? After much study and searching I must conclude that the Bible doesn't specifically say that Christians can have demons, but there are a number of references that indicate it very strongly.

- (James 3:10,14,15) James writing to and about Christians said: *"...This wisdom does not descend from above, but is earthly, sensual, demonic."* It is obvious that these Christians were drawing from demonic sources, as well as from the Spirit of God.
- 2 Corinthians 11:3,4 *"...as the serpent deceived Eve by his craftiness.... or if you receive a different spirit which you have not received...."* A different spirit is a contrast to the Holy Spirit. So it indicates an unholy spirit or demon. This was also written to Christians.
- Ephesians 4:26,27 *"...do not let the sun go down on your wrath, nor give place to the devil."* The word translated "place" is the Greek word "topos" which means spot, space,

or location. This verse is saying not to give ground. Don't give a foothold in your life to the devil. Paul is talking to Christians, so obviously it is possible for Christians to give place to the devil.

Even with these notes there are many who object to the idea of a Christian being influenced by a demon.

Objection Number One - Once a person is saved, he belongs to God and that the Lord would never allow some other power to control, influence, or in any way harm that which belongs to Him.

Response - God has set up certain laws, laws of nature and laws of the Spirit. Disobedience to those laws brings certain effects. For everything, there is a cause and an effect. If you step off a ten-story building, you will fall. In such a situation, you would be dealing with the law of gravity, and God will not turn off the law of gravity just because you are ignorant enough to defy it. The same is true of His spiritual laws. If we don't obey God's laws, we suffer the consequences.

- This does not in any way diminish the grace or goodness of God. All of Gods gifts have boundaries or laws. When we violate a boundary, like the boundary of gravity, we suffer the consequences. If a person doesn't recognize and provide for the body's need for rest and nourishment, he will become susceptible to weakness and sickness. Therefore, when we choose to violate one of Gods boundaries, whether natural or spiritual, there are consequences that we must face.
- The Christian must also remember that even though his spirit has been changed, his body is not yet redeemed. Romans 7 and 8 give us a clear picture of the struggle between the flesh and the spirit of a believer. Romans 8:7 says the carnal mind is enmity against God and can't even be subject to God's law. Romans 8:23 says, *"we also, who have the firstfruits of the Spirit, even we ourselves groan within ourselves, eagerly waiting for the adoption, the redemption of our body."*

- Therefore, even though we as Christians are the temples of the Holy Spirit, we live in unredeemed bodies. We make the choice in our will, in the area of our soul, whether or not we are going to walk according to our redeemed spirit or according to our unredeemed flesh. If we choose to walk according to the spirit, we are well protected. If we choose to walk according to the desires of the flesh, we open the door to sin and demonic activity.
- People who believe that receiving Jesus is all there is to "salvation" are missing a lot. Confessing Jesus as our Savior is the starting point, not the finish line. Once a person has made this step, he must then learn to walk according to the truths in God's word. He must learn to follow God's guidelines to possess the land of his own soul (mind, will, emotions) and body.

Objection number two – A Christian is the temple of God, and a holy God would not share His dwelling place with anything unholy.

Response - In the first two chapters of Job we find Satan himself coming into God's presence. He is the epitome of evil, and yet he entered the presence of God.

- Then we see in Colossians 3:5 where Paul is addressing believers. He said, *"Therefore put to death your members which are on the earth: fornication, uncleanness, passion, evil desire, and covetousness, which is idolatry."* Are these things holy? No. Were they and are they found in believers? Yes. They exist in the temple where the Holy Spirit also dwells.
- Remember that the Hebrew temple had three courts. The Holy of Holies is representative of our spirit. The Holy Place is representative of our soul. The Outer Court, our body (flesh). A demon cannot inhabit the Christian's spirit (the Holy of Holies), but it can inhabit the Christian's body/flesh (the Outer Court). In Galatians 5:17, we read that "the flesh sets its desire against the spirit, and the spirit against

the flesh; for these are in opposition to one another." The soul (mind, will, and emotion) is the Holy Place, and is the zone of conflict between the spirit and the flesh. The soul reflects that which controls it.
- Let's look at a scripture that we are very familiar with in Matthew 18. It should throw additional light on this thought. Matthew 18:19 "Again I say to you that if two of you agree on earth concerning anything that they ask, it will be done for them by My Father in heaven."
- Usually we consider this to refer to two different people, but I believe it can also refer to two different parts of the same person. What do you think the flesh and the spirit are in conflict over? They war for control of the soul. Your will makes the decisions of your life. If it agrees with the spirit, you have two in agreement. If it agrees with the flesh, you have two in agreement. Can you see why there is such a battle for your mind, will, and emotions?
- So, the spirit is the dwelling place of the Holy Spirit. It lines up with His character and produces the fruit of His character. However, the flesh is subject to sin and therefore to the influence of demons (Galatians 5:19-21). The soul can be persuaded either way. It can obey the spirit and force submission of the flesh, or it can agree with the flesh and cut off the work of the spirit.

Objection number three: "Can you show me any place in the Bible where a saved person had a demon?"

Response - Well, no, not in such terminology. Nevertheless, neither can you prove that many of the people in the Bible who had demons were not saved. The Bible rarely speaks of the experience of salvation as a finished act. It is always ongoing. Philippians 2:12 exhorts us to work out our own salvation with fear and trembling. The word "salvation" comes from the Greek word "sozo" which means "to deliver, to save, to protect." The word is most frequently used in the present active tense showing that salvation is presently being worked out in the believer's life.

- The Bible does not speak about salvation of the flesh. We will eventually receive new bodies, and these we are now living in will perish. It speaks of the spirit being born again. When the Bible speaks of salvation, it is nearly always in reference to the soul and in terms of continuing or future action. Let's look at a couple of examples.
- I Peter 1:3-9 *"...who are kept by the power of God through faith for salvation ready to be revealed in the last time... receiving the end of your faith - the salvation of your souls."*
- James 1:21 *"...receive with meekness the implanted word, which is able to save your souls."* (Other references to salvation of the soul: Matthew 16:25,26; Mark 8:35-37; Hebrews 10:39. Related references: I Peter 2:11; 3 John 2; I Peter 1:22; Hebrews 13:7; I Peter 2:25) We can correctly say that we have been saved, are being saved and will be saved. The spirit is "regenerated" when you receive Jesus as Savior, but the Bible doesn't use that terminology concerning the *soul*. It most frequently speaks of the *soul* as being *saved*.
- John 3:3-6 *"...unless one is born again he cannot see the kingdom of God...That which is born of the flesh is flesh, and that which is born of the Spirit is spirit."* Note especially the last phrase, *"that which is born of the Spirit is spirit."* Therefore, when we receive Jesus as our Savior, our spirit is *born again* or *regenerated*. It is more than saved. It is recreated, totally new.
- 1 Peter 1:23 says, *"having been born again, not of corruptible seed but incorruptible, through the word of God which lives and abides forever."* The spirit is born of the incorruptible seed. The perfection of God resides in it. It is a completely new being, perfect in character. But the perfect character of the spirit of a man can only manifest itself to the degree that the soul will come into agreement with it and allow that manifestation. The more the soul is delivered (saved) from the influence of the flesh and the devil, the more the life of the believer will exemplify the life of Christ, which resides in his spirit. The essence of salvation is that it is completely

accomplished by the work of Jesus; entered into through the new birth experience, and is progressively worked out in our personal relationship with the Lord. Remember that the spirit is made new when we receive Jesus, but the body and soul are not. This is an example of positional truth and experiential truth. The positional truth is that we have been saved, more accurately our spirits have been regenerated. Experientially, we have to walk it out. Basically deliverance (sozo) is *"salvation."* As we minister to people, we are instruments of salvation for the Holy Spirit, by being a willing vessel to be used to help others be delivered from the works of the enemy and work out their salvation.

Now hopefully we have answers to objections that people might use to say that Christians can't have a demon and, therefore, don't need deliverance. They can and often do. We'll be explaining how the demons get in and give a workable pattern for getting them out in later lessons.

Is it possible to Start Over?

Diagnostic Questions – If you were to die right now, do you have the assurance that you would go to heaven? Suppose you were to stand before God today and He were to say to you, "Why should I let you into My kingdom?" - What would you say to Him?

Prognosis – Considering the three basic parts of man, the spirit is re-created instantly, but the body and soul are progressive in their restoration process.

Remedy - The vital connection to Jesus is a decision with profound consequences, therefore should be considered carefully. Complete understanding is not a pre-requisite for this commitment.

Salvation - The Starting Point

Strong's definition of "sozo": is "to save, i.e. deliver or protect (literally or figuratively): heal, preserve, save (self), do well, be (make) whole."

In Matthew 1:21, it says that Jesus came to save His people from their sins. It is from the result of sin that we must be delivered, protected, healed, preserved, made whole, saved. The result of sin is separation from God, which is death. Remember, "the wages of sin is death." Death is not only the final termination of physical life. It is also manifested in demonic bondage, slavery to our sin nature, sickness, and the destruction of our bodies, our character and our relationships. These are all areas from which we must be delivered.

Salvation continued - The Calling of God

I Thessalonians 5:23 & 24 "Now may the God of peace Himself sanctify you entirely; and may your spirit and soul and body be preserved complete, without blame at the coming of our Lord Jesus Christ. Faithful is He who calls you, and He also will bring it to pass."

So, God is not only faithful to call you, but He is able to bring it to pass. He calls you, enables you to be born again and then, step by step, brings about your salvation or deliverance from the things that represent death within you.

Salvation the Process

One bit of hope for us as Christians can be found in Jeremiah 2:21. It says that the seed of the vine that God has planted within you is faithful. Peter says we have been born again of incorruptible seed (1 Peter 1:23). Anything that is not consistent with the character of God within you, according to Jeremiah 2, is a degenerate root of a foreign vine. That is a corruptible seed. It is not you. Many times we attribute things to our own character because we see shortcomings in us, but that is not our character. This is the destruction of the enemy. This is the junk of Satan that entered into Adam and Eve through the fall. This is not who we are, because we have been recreated in Christ Jesus, and we have a faithful vine within us. It will come up. It will bear fruit. It will be complete. Anything to the contrary is a degenerate shoot of a foreign vine, and it's not you. So that is to take condemnation off of you from the start.

When a person is truly *born again*, God's incorruptible seed is in implanted in that person. The spirit of that person has been totally made new, reborn. His spirit is saved. But *salvation* is an ongoing process (Philippians 2:12; 1 Thessalonians 5:8,9). It is to cover every aspect of our being, spirit, soul and body. The ultimate purpose of God for the individual is that he be made completely whole in every aspect of life. This must start with the *new birth*. This gives the potential for all of the rest of *salvation*.

Salvation by Grace through Faith

Every step in the process of salvation, including deliverance, healing, being made whole, all the things involved in salvation, must be accomplished by grace through faith. So the *divine enablement* of God, which is grace, is worked out by the application of our faith. Faith is the vehicle by which we use the grace that God gives us to work out our salvation. So we see right now that our salvation, our deliverance, is an activity. It isn't a passive thing. It is ongoing and being worked out by our faith. We always take hold of the things purchased for us by Christ through faith.

I Peter 1:9 "...obtaining the outcome of your faith, the salvation of your souls."

The Ministry

Now as we begin to minister to people, we must understand that it is that incorruptible seed of God within that makes all of the rest of their deliverance or salvation possible. The first step in salvation is to be born again. The process of salvation begins with new birth. New birth is number one, our access to the things of God, and, numbers two, our potential for salvation in every area of our life. Without a new birth you have no access or potential for any salvation experience.

Is the Person Born Again?

Initially determine if the person is born again. (Read John 3:1-7 and John 1:13 to see that new birth is the beginning process.) Here we are only looking for the new birth experience. We are not checking for the process of salvation. There may have been very little salvation in this person's life, and many aspects of their personality and their character may still need to be delivered. If that were not the case, they probably wouldn't be coming to us for help. But we want to find out if the source for that help is there; that access to their potential is present within them. This is present in the form of the Spirit of God, implanted within them at new birth. Have they truly been born again?

Discerning the New Birth Experience

Romans 10:9 says, "...that if you confess (literally, "to speak the same thing") with your mouth Jesus as Lord, and believe (literally, "to trust in, rely upon, and adhere to") in your heart that God raised Him from the dead, you shall be saved (literally, "delivered")." It is possible for people to say all sorts of things without really believing them. It is possible to say the sinner's prayer in hopes of escaping hell with no real commitment to the Lordship of Jesus. A person may know almost nothing about what it means to make Jesus his Savior and Lord, but may truly be born again because the desire of his heart was an honest desire that the Lord come in and change his life. Another person may have a lot of knowledge of what the Bible has to say about salvation and may have said the right things for reasons that seem to benefit himself without any desire for a real relationship with Jesus.

Only the Lord knows what a person believes in his heart at the time that he confesses with his mouth. Only the Lord can read the sincerity of the confession and the commitment. You and I cannot judge and cannot know unless the Lord Himself reveals it to us by the Spirit. So in all types of ministry, you must be spiritually aware.

The "New Birth" Cannot Be Intellectually Discerned

You can't intellectually discern whether or not a person actually has a connection with God by asking him questions. It is good to ask him about his new birth experience and let him share it. As he shares it, he will be speaking his experience, and it is very likely that he will be releasing a spiritual atmosphere as he recounts what Christ has done for him. You must be tuned in to and discerning the atmosphere that he is releasing as he speaks of his new birth experience. You must be spiritually aware. You must be able to discern by the spirit if this person has an honest commitment to the Lord or not. The person himself may not realize that he is only involved in some religious activity and has not committed himself to a living relationship. He may be trying to follow somebody's law and never have experienced "…the Spirit Himself bears witness with our spirit that we are children of God." (Romans 8:16)

You are not to judge the person, but if there is any doubt as to the sincerity of his commitment or the reality of his born again experience, ask him some questions about his willingness to allow the Lord to direct his life. You may then need to pray with him to be born again.

Dealing with Heart Issues Requires Commitment

If there is an indication that this person is wanting easy answers to his problems without commitment on his part, you will have to be very sensitive as to what to do next. Jesus healed all who came and asked, so it is possible to minister to someone who is not born again or is not willing to allow Jesus to be Lord of his life. God may want to express His love for that person in some way through ministry. But as a general rule, ministry without commitment doesn't have lasting effects. For a life to really be changed, the person must come to a place of real commitment. Usually desire precedes desperation, which precedes commitment. But understand, desperation does not equal commitment.

So your first step in ministry is to find out where this person is in relation to the Lord. Is he really born again? Is the life of God within, giving the potential for real lasting change in his life? Is he willing to allow God to do what needs to be done? If the answer is "no" to any of these questions, it is unlikely that you will want to take the next step in ministry… or maybe you do. So remember ministry is always to be guided by the Holy Spirit, not by a set of rule or regulations.

Soul Mapping – part 1

Diagnostic Questions – Do you struggle with repeated patterns of destructive behavior? Do you have destructive behavior patterns similar to those of your parents or grandparents? What "bad habits" plague you the most?
Prognosis – Iniquity, transgression, and sin are a progressive trilogy that results in destructive behavior patterns. Due to the "invisibility" of iniquity and transgressions, destructive behavior is usually not interrupted until the final stage of "sin."
Remedy – there is a three-part remedy: (1) confession (2) circumcision of heart (3) baptism of fire

---

A map is a critical tool for navigation… whether in the air or on the ground, "GPS" or the old standard paper map, maps are enlightening for direction. Where am I? How did I get here? Where am I going? How do I get out of here? In this chapter we will begin to discuss a process we call *"soul mapping."*

When people come in for counseling, we don't see the roots. The most obvious thing we see is the behavior that they are producing in their lives. But we must see that there is a cause and effect for this behavior. Without understanding the cause, if we only adjust the effect, then our efforts will be like "putting a band-aid on cancer." For decades, behavioral science has studied specific behaviors endeavoring to define the cause and effect of each. This understanding does not produce the cure, but does give direction for potential cure. Without understand the "cause" we will never really get to "the root" of where we are…or where we might end up if the behavior continues uninterrupted. The best we can do without this understanding is "behavior modification."

For this study we are beginning our *mapping* by dealing with the "roots". Discovering these roots will frequently answer the question, "Where did this behavior come from?" or "Why am I like this?"

So what are the *roots* of most destructive behavior? The first *root* we are going to talk about is *iniquity.*

Iniquity

Exodus 34:7 says that there are three things that God forgives. "Who keeps loving kindness for thousands, who forgives *iniquity, transgression,* and *sin*…"

God forgives *iniquity, transgression* and *sin*…but they are different. What is passed down to the third and fourth generation? *Iniquity.* What is *iniquity? Iniquity* literally means the "bent, propensity, or desire." There are things in our life that we bend to or lean toward… things towards which we have a predisposition.

So *iniquity* is a wrong or destructive *"bent"* which can potentially pass down from generation to generation. **Transgression** (Exodus 34:7) takes place the moment your *will consents to the desire.* In that moment a *decision* is made. The *sin* takes place when an *action* or *behavior* occurs. So here is the *"Progression of Behavior": Bent/ Desire Decision Behavior.*

Desires fall into four general categories: **Natural Desires** (hunger, sleep, etc.), **God Placed Desires** (for example, the "zeal of God" has "passion" as a primary ingredient), **Demonically Incited Desires** and **Iniquities.**

Iniquities can only find expression in the vacuum of faith. Because *iniquities* germinate only in the absence of faith, the enemy's plan is to get us to disconnect our faith. This strategy begins with a *lie.* Basically, there are *three lies that the enemy presents*… only three… but in varied forms and fashions. These lies are the same lies found in the early chapters of the book of Genesis (the first book of the Bible).

Lie Number One – *"God doesn't really care about me."* One of the enemy's most common and most frequently used lies is one that insinuates that God is withholding something good from you… that somehow, you are incomplete… that God doesn't really care about you.

Lie Number Two – *"Life is unfair."* The enemy communicates this lie through circumstances that seem to convey that there are no real consequences to wrong choices and wrong behavior.

Lie Number Three – *"You don't measure up."* This lie diminishes who God says we are, and attempts to make us feel that we are somehow disfigured or not really in God's image and likeness. It screams that we are less than who God says we are, therefore, we need to do something extra to achieve that place of *likeness*. The result is a life spent trying to *"measure up."*

These three lies speak to us primarily through **circumstances** and the **careless words** of others… seeking to distract our eyes from Him to something that we have to do to bridge the gap of trust.

Understanding these basic three lies will enable us to recognize the *faith-destruction* tactics. Working with these three lies are five **Fantasy Drives**. When a **"God seed"** (anything God puts into the imagination by word, thought, action, etc.) is fertilized by the *imagination*, it will result in **Vision**. Other **"seeds"** (not God seeds) combined with *imagination* resulting in a *fantasy*… a *disconnection* from reality. In Ezekiel 28:14-19, God is speaking to Lucifer who became Satan and said, "By the multitude of your iniquities, in the unrighteousness of your trade, you profane your sanctuaries…" Then in Isaiah 14:12-14 in the discourse of about Lucifer, we have demonstrated the **Five Fantasy Drives.**

The first Fantasy Drive says, *"I can do it!"* This drive is one of **self-reliance.** This drive is usually spurred on by the *pain* of lack of approval. This person is usually a driven and successful person. A person compelled by this fantasy drive will be one who will go to all ends to achieve success. Deep within their subconscious is the equation that only if I can be successful, then I will have others approval… and the converse equation, *failure means disapproval*. This is a *pain* driven fantasy.

The second Fantasy Drive says, "**Get out of my way!**" The focus of this drive is one of *selfish ambition* and *self-promotion*. This person will not give regard for others along their climb to the top. Usually grounded in a *broken trust*, this drive will make one *controlling* and seemingly *uncaring* about others. This is a *pride* driven fantasy.

The third Fantasy Drive says, "*No one will tell me what to do.*" Driven by the *fear of rejection* this drive will tend to produce an *independent* person; one who frequently *withdraws* and *isolates* from others as a defensive posture. This person will frequently have a string of *authority issues* in their lives, their marriage, and their jobs. This is a *fear/pain* driven fantasy.

The fourth fantasy drive says, "*Look at me!*" This fantasy drive is usually found in the person that struggles with the part of their Identity that is centered around the "***uniqueness factor***." This person will overtly seek the "lime light." Their desire is for fame, popularity and name recognition. Many who approach the fields of politics and the arts like theatre find themselves caught by this fantasy drive. This fantasy drive is rarely consciously fear or pain driven. Due to the lack of an *anchored identity*, they will most frequently *not be in touch with the cause of the drive. This is an approval driven fantasy.*

The fifth fantasy drive says, "*I will be what I want to be!*" This fantasy drive seeks to have a *self-determined* identity. While all of us have the ability to be whom we desire, this drive escalates this process by not receiving input... especially input from God. This is a *self-established* purpose, not a God given purpose that can lead to "destiny." *This is an independent/pride driven fantasy.*

Again, note that these five fantasy drives all focus on self: Self Reliance, Self Ambition, Self Promotion, Self Relating, and Self Display. These fantasy drives are frequently unconscious motivations. One thing that we must remember is that God looks at the heart. It is man who looks at the outside of a person. If you **desire** to sin, it is as important to God that you *repent* (repent means literally "to change the mind") of the *desire* as it is that you *repent* of the *act*. So a wrong desire of the heart is as much sin in the eyes of God as the acting out of that wrong desire. In the repentance process, God is not only interested in *what* we do, but also in *why* we do it. The *why* is our motivation? When we understand *why* we act, we'll discover many benign actions are conceived from wrong motives.

Many of the good things that we do are born of a wrong desire, of iniquity that is in our heart. We all have legitimate needs in our lives. When we try to get these needs fulfilled apart from our relationship with God, we find ourselves acting out the iniquity of our hearts. The need is not wrong; it is legitimate, but the manner we seek to fulfill it is wrong, following the dictates of our desires or iniquities instead of seeking God.

Even the desire for acceptance can involve iniquity. For example, some people perform humanitarian endeavors to gain self-acceptance, so they can achieve a sense of worth or a feeling of value within themselves. It is only because they lack that worth, because they are not receiving that acceptance from God, that they go and do what is seemingly a good work. God desires that the need for acceptance be met the same way He desires to meet all our needs, even though *He uses people*, ultimately the need is met through relationship with Him.

He wants to do this before we ever launch out into any kind of ministry. If a heart-need is not met by Him, within the context of God given relationships and settings, it will not really be met. It will be false and leave a sense of emptiness. Iniquity is the most difficult thing to deal with because it is hidden and invisible. Some of the other destructive behavior (sin) aspects that we are going to talk about are very obvious, but iniquity is often hidden and secretive in our hearts. That's why *self-realization* (honesty) and *self-disclosure* (transparency) are such an important aspect to the restoration process.

Dealing with Iniquities

There are three keys to dealing with iniquities:

- The first is simple. Just as **confession** is the key to dealing with sin, it is also the key to activating *forgiveness* concerning iniquities. Remember, the word "Confess" means literally

"to speak the same as." "To speak the same" means to say what God says about what you have just done. God says three things: (1) That desire is Iniquity (2) Change how you look at it... to excuse it or explain it... ***own it!*** (3) You are forgiven! Penitence is not necessary!
- The second is that special tool called the "***circumcision of the heart.***" This is a spiritual application of a physical term. From the prophet Jeremiah, through the writings of the Apostle Paul, we find this application of the term.
- The third tool for dealing with iniquities is "***the baptism of fire.***" In Isaiah chapter six, we find a servant of God in a precarious position. Upon realizing that he was in some type of destructive behavior system, he cried out to God. "Woe is me, for I am ruined! Because I am a man of unclean lips, and I live among a people of unclean lips... Then one of the seraphim flew to me, with a burning coal in his hand, that he had taken from the altar with tongs. And he touched my mouth with it and said, "Behold, this has touched your lips; and your iniquity is taken away (literally "has been turned off"), and your sin is forgiven."

This fire for the *believer* is the same found in the Baptism of Fire... part of the impartation of what is frequently called, the *Baptism or Filling of the Holy Spirit*. This is a *spiritual experience* where a person connects to the Holy Spirit in a real and dynamic way.

- A fourth practical tool for dealing with "desires" is "***Re-direction.***" When wrong desires are a pattern or "habit" it is helpful to identify an alternative "desire" or "thought direction" that can be substituted or "redirected" each time the destructive habit/thought begins. For example, during times of grief, people tend to re-direct by eating, or working, or some sport participation.

Transgression

Now let's look at transgression, a second part of the *"Progression of Behavior."* Remember Exodus 34:7 says that God forgives iniquity, transgression and sin. You might say, "Aren't iniquity and transgression just sin? What's the difference?"

In the Hebrew, "transgression" means a "revolt (national, moral, or religious)" and it is translated, "rebellion, sin, transgression, trespass." It comes from a root word that means, "to break away from just authority". It is an *aggressive choice to action*. In order to transgress, one must literally *choose* to revolt and rebel. It is always a revolt or rebellion against a set authority.

We cannot *accidentally* transgress. This is something that we do *decidedly and on purpose*. The things we do as Christians, which we don't realize are *sin*, probably won't cause us a lot of problem in our lives. Why? The exhortation of 1John says simply, "walk in the light at He is in the light…" Simply put, do what you know to do! The things that cause us trouble are the things that the Holy Spirit has convicted us of, but we have either ignored or refused to deal with. The most violent of destructive behavior systems are going to be the result of transgression, the revolt against a set authority in his life. It may be rebellion against parents, rebellion against legal authority, or rebellion against the Holy Spirit. A person can get into very serious bondage and trouble by transgression. **Transgressions are premeditated acts of the will,** and such transgressions will form the most difficult of bondages in a person's life.

What comprises a decision? How is a decision made? There are several ingredients to most decisions.

1. Most decisions involve a gathering or inventory of information, or *An Information Inventory.* This involves counsel from others (both desired and unsolicited), research, promptings from the Holy Spirit… all along with some sort of *"pro & con" assessment*. This process is usually a conscious one for the first time, then less and less conscious when the same or similar decision is repeated.

2. Most decisions involve *perception*. Remember that your perception also has several ingredients:

   - **Projection** – what another person desires for you to perceive
   - **Reality** – what is actual or true... realizing there is both a spiritual and a natural reality
   - **Negative experiences** – those which wound and demean the value of a person
   - **Positive experiences** – those which reinforce and build-up the value of a person
   - **What you believe** will also affect your perception
   - **Circumstances, present pressures and realities** will affect your perception

3. Decisions are affected by the platform of needs & desires. When "*urgency*" or "*desperation*" is present, the decisions may be premature or incomplete in their processing. These are frequently fear driven decisions... the fear of loss, the fear of death, etc.
4. *Judgments* will affect your decisions. The very things that you despise, which you have judged another for, are the very things that you find yourself deciding for. This is the paradox of a judgment... a sort of boom-a-rang effect.
5. *Wounds* will affect your decisions. Wounds have an ability to distort and skew the thought *processes* as well as the *perception*.
6. *Unhealthy relationships* have the ability to affect the decision making process. For example, when a mother is controlling or overbearing with her children, frequently the children develop a type of "co-dependency" during their adolescent years. Another stereotypical relationship, which is an incubator for codependency, is the *dominant* spouse... this is a relationship defined by a *superior and inferior,* or a *dominant and subordinate*.
7. *Dysfunctional or Destructive Behavior Systems*. These are systems of behavior that have developed past the decision-making part of the process (remember, Bent/Desire — Decision — Behavior) and the will is only infrequently involved in the

behavior. This progression is from *bent/desire* or *need...* to *behavior*. Notice the *volition* has been circumvented... and the behavior no longer requires a *choice*.

Dealing with Unhealthy Decisions

1. ***Forgiveness is always the foundation*** for dealing with issues of the heart. So what does God forgive? He forgives *iniquity*...our errant desires. He forgives *transgressions*...our wrong choices. He forgives us when we *rebel* against Him. He forgives *sin* of every kind, which means He forgives even the things we do that we don't realize are sins. This covers just about everything that we could possibly do. Is there anything that is outside the realm of God's forgiveness? There is nothing that God will not forgive, if we will only trust Him.

Another practical in the process of forgiveness is the healing of the wounds in the heart. This is frequently begun with a counselor or helper "speaking forgiveness aloud" to the one violated. "I forgive you!" "You are forgiven!" These are powerful statements that frequently open the door to further healing of the heart.

2. A second key to interrupting wrong decision-making patterns is to ***change the perception***. Change how you *view* the situation and circumstance.

There is a biblical word that encompasses this process. It is the word "repentance." It literally means, "to change the mind". This step is part of what our *"Introduction"* calls the ***"God look."*** Sometimes this step is aided by a counselor using Biblical principles and truth... "mentoring" new paradigms into the struggling individual. Frequently this process involves *"deciding"* against the *"desires."* You may *see* what God *says*, but due to other heart issues like wounds, you do not "feel" or "desire" the change... but seeing the "big picture," you ***choose against your own feelings and desires***.

It is also at this step, where the love of God needs to be reinforced. It is very difficult to **change the perceptions** without a sensing of God's love and kindness toward the person. Without feeling loved and having a purpose in life, there is little desire to change. But when we are convinced that another loves us, especially when our behavior is not lovely, we are easily persuaded by them to change. That's why the Bible says "kindness of God leads us to repentance." There is something about love in the face of our *un-lovely-ness*, that breaks our hearts and moves us to desire change.

3. When Destructive Behavior Systems are ***chronic*** (involuntary repetition), there is frequently a need for *"**deliverance**"* to take place. During the process of repeated decisions, there is a *"**surrendering of the will**"* which allow demonic influences to take over the decision making process. This step will be discussed in a later chapter.
4. The setting of ***boundaries*** is an important step in the recovery of a "co-dependant" person. Boundaries make room for health and healing to progress. As with any part of our anatomy, after it has been healed, a "therapy" is needed to rebuild the weakened area. Even so in the decision making process, there is a taking back of the *right* (authority) and *process* of making our own decisions.

Dealing with the Problems

Getting rid of sin is a matter of *confession* and *repentance*. However, different roots of bondage and sin need different approaches in ministry in addition to confession and repentance.

Sin:
1. The person needs to confess the sin, and receive forgiveness.

Transgression:
1. May require deliverance.

Iniquity:
1. Cut soul-ties at both ends, from the source as well as to the person.
2. Renounce all ground taken through *iniquity*. Take back the ground. These verbal reinforcements are important in activating new thought & understanding processes.
3. Share the joy of water baptism asking God to circumcise the heart.
4. Ask God to baptize them with fire. Remember, it is this "passion" (fire) of God that really "checks" the activity of wrong desires. It is similar to how love restrains infidelity.
5. Ask God to give them *His desires* in place of the iniquities.
6. Begin to discover and embrace *who God says you are*. It is frequently helpful to speak and confess these truths as realities, as you begin to engage *His perspective* of you.

Did My Daddy Make Me Do It?

Diagnostic Questions – Do you have destructive behavior patterns that run in your family? Do you have habits that are the same as those of your parents or grandparents? Do certain physical or emotional diseases *run* in your family?
Prognosis – Frequently trans-generational behavior (destructive behavior) is due to "iniquity transference."
Remedy - (1) Discover of the Root (2) Separating the root from the person (3) Reorienting (renewing) towards a new behavior

So iniquity is the *desire* to sin, and can be passed down from generation to generation. We often ask God to take away the bad desires in our hearts. To much dismay they remain day after day. It is not because God does not care or is unable to answer our prayers? He desires to see each of us work through our heart issues. Over the years I have come to believe God knows best! He is always in control and He is very able. I also believe He always has our best interest at heart. He would rather allow each of us to see the "disease" in our hearts and then provides the remedy for that "disease."

Remember, it is this *iniquity* (desire) that passes from generation to generation. This is sometimes referred to as "ancestral bondages." To paint a picture of this trans-generational iniquity, we will use the imaginary Jones family. Great Grandpa Joe struggled with the iniquity of adultery for many years. He often read Playboy magazines and daily allowed his mind to be consumed by lustful thoughts. One day he yields to his weakness and acts on those lustful thoughts. He commits adultery. The acting out of his hidden desires gave the iniquity a cause or a way to root itself in the Jones family. Remember that Proverbs tells us "a curse without a cause can not light."

Next in line is Grandpa Bill and John Senior. Both Bill and John Senior spent their life fighting lustful thoughts and tendencies. Although neither man ever acted on his lustful desires, the iniquity of adultery is still alive and strong in the Jones family. Years pass and now John Junior is facing his early twenties and constantly finds himself in topless bars. He tells himself over and over he is going to break this bad habit, but something so strong always pulls him back. John junior soon finds himself in bed with woman after woman as he acts out the iniquity passed down from great grandpa Joe.

Now, everything starts over in the Jones family only this time it will be John Junior's children and grandchildren that have to struggle with adultery. Exodus 20:5 says, "visiting the iniquity of the fathers on the children; on the third and the fourth generations…" As we have seen in the Jones family iniquity is passed down as far as the fourth generation. The bent towards adultery existed from great grandpa Joe to John Junior. Does this mean that the Jones family will inevitably commit adultery? Are they are doomed to fail? What's the Remedy?

- So how does John junior get rid of the strong pull towards adultery
- Confess the sins of the past generations (as much as are known)
- Take responsibility for personal cooperation
- Break spiritual power sin has had in the family
- Reclaim stolen and lost areas the family has given to Satan

So Junior might pray something like this: "Lord I see the lines of sin that run in my family and I confess the lust, perversion, pornography, and adultery as sin. I take responsibility for the role I have played in allowing these sins to continue in my family. Today I am choosing to change the course my family is taking. In Jesus Name I break the power of this line of iniquity. Today I take back every

Issues

piece of God's destiny and His provision for our family. Thank you for your forgiveness and grace. In Jesus Name, Amen."

- Does John junior need to know every member of his family and every sin committed in order to address the iniquities he struggles with personally?

Frequently the only way that we are going to be able to find these ancestral connections is by the revelation of the Holy Spirit. Words of knowledge and other gifts of the Spirit are necessary to dig out the truth. Many times the person will not even know much about his ancestors. The Lord must reveal the areas where we need to minister. Therefore our responsibility is simply to "walk in the light", which means, be responsible for what we know, and God will take care of the rest.

- How can John junior prevent this strong lustful desire from continuing in his children even after he has committed adultery himself?

Confessing our sin is normal part of daily Christian living. It is not a one time thing, or a once a week thing. Each time we sin, it is our responsibility to process that sin in such a way that we come to "agreement with God" (the literally definition of "confess") that (1) it is sin (2) I change my perspective concerning it (3) I am forgiven.

There are some other keys that aid in maintaining the newly acquired freedom

1. Establish and maintain clear boundaries (see chapter twelve).
2. Set up an "accountability" relationship – this is a relationship with someone you trust and you know loves you…someone who will "get in your face" over your daily "successes" and "failures."

3. Support groups are helpful when you have difficulty processing circumstances or feelings.

Now let's look at this idea of "heritage" or "trans-generational iniquity" on a different level. Let's look at it from a cultural or national level. We find whole cultures very prone or bent toward certain weaknesses. For example, we will find attitude of poverty resting on whole cultures. Sometimes we even find things like lying or cheating so prevalent that, in the eyes of the people, there is nothing wrong with such behavior. They consider it normal. Other cultures consider laziness to be the norm. It seems very hard to extricate these people out of that type of situation. But, if we can break these ancestral curses off them, we will begin to see them set free.

One day I received a telephone call from a pastor. He informed me that he had a problem and wondered if I could come to his church for a small conference and discuss the problem. When I arrived I was taken to dinner by the pastor. During dinner he began to unfold for me the dilemma that was plaguing him. His church was struggling with finances. It seems to him that they had been struggling since the beginning with the problem of finances. His church was in a border city... on the border of Texas and Mexico. The church consisted primarily of Hispanic families. After spending a lot of time looking at the financial records, I began to pray and ask God to show me the cause of the financial problems. As I began to pray, I began to see a problem with the culture.

The Hispanic culture is commonly known as a "matriarchal" culture. This simply means that in the family unit, it is usually the mother or the grandmother that is honored as the "head" of the family. The only problem is that God sets for the father, not the mother, as the head of a family. This illegal headship inverts the authority, and leads to "dishonor" for the true head... the father. A close study of the cause and effect of "poverty" will find "poverty" closely tied to "dishonor". When I began to teach this principle to the church, I was amazed at the response. The weeping and contrition among the people for the dishonor they had shown to their leaders, fathers, pastors, etc. The results were simply astounding. Within a few short weeks the finances of the church began to turn around. What had once been a cultural behavior system, had been interrupted and changed.

People of one culture are not inherently better or worse. It is simply their trans-generational behavior system that holds them. This type of behavior is a very strong thing. If the iniquity is there, the enemy will take full advantage to tempt and seduce in that area. Let's look at something that Peter had to say in this area.

> I Peter 2:9-10 "...you are a chosen race...once you were not a people..."

What I want you to see is that "once you were not a people". When was this, that you were "not a people"? Before you were *born again*, you were not a people. What this means is that God does not recognize races and nationalities as we look at them. To Him there are two groups, those who are in His family and those who are not.

Then Peter says "Beloved, I urge you as aliens and strangers to abstain from fleshly lusts, which wage war against the soul."(1Peter 2:11) You are to be an alien or stranger to the world's attitudes. Look at the problem of pride in heritage. There are people whose trans-generational behavior cannot be broken because of pride in heritage. Perhaps they are proud of their Jewish heritage, proud of their Spanish heritage, proud of the Indian heritage, and this identity attachment blinds them to the inherent weaknesses of their culture.

Our natural heritage should neither bring us pride or shame. Understand that we have but one heritage, if we are children of God. We were "not a people" before we became children of God. We didn't have a heritage in the eyes of God. But now we are a people. Our heritage is in the family and kingdom of God.

According to this, we are now aliens to what we once were. Once we were Mexican but now we are children of God; once we were German, but now we are children of God; once we were Jewish, but now we are children of God. 2 Corinthians 5:20 says we are "ambassadors for Christ". Our heritage now goes beyond anything we could have ever received in what we once were. We are now "a people". We have been formed into a new race. Our heritage is in God. If we would forget the traditions and heritages of the past and find out what our heritage and tradition is in God, we would come together in a common union as the body of Christ. In Christ we all have the same heritage. We are a common people, not by race or color, but by the Spirit.

Soul Mapping – part II
(Destructive Behavior Systems)

Diagnostic Questions – Do you have repeated patterns of destructive behavior that you have been unable to break? Do you have bad habits? If so, what are they?

Prognosis – There are systems and schemes of destructive behavior that consume areas of our hearts and lives. Unless these schemes are interrupted, our hearts will never be restored.

Remedy – Understanding Cause and Effect is a tremendous aid to a permanent cure for Destructive Behaviors. *Soul Mapping* is a tool to aid in this discovery.

One the greatest challenges of any counselor is the unraveling of a life of *destructive patterns of behavior*. Where the **effect** is most obvious, the **cause** is frequently hidden under layers of choices. These choices give way to *schemes* **or** *systems*. It is these *schemes* or *systems* that counselors must learn to interrupt.

As this chapter unfolds, I want to begin by noting how we learn to fight these *systems.*

1. We must learn to *fight by priority*.
   - We must learn to war over our own heart. (1Corinthians 6:19-20).
   - We must learn to war over our family. (Ephesians 5).
   - We must learn to war over our local church (1 Corinthians 3:16).
   - We must learn to war over other expressions and situations outside the local church. (John 14:2).

2. We must learn to *fight wars spiritually.* The apostle Paul said in 2 Corinthians 2:11, "Do not be ignorant concerning the *schemes* (systems) of the enemy." A *scheme* is the opposite of a *strategy*. This will be the subject of this chapter.

3. We must learn to *fight wars generationally.* God is a God of the "multi-generations." God most frequently presented Himself as "The God of your fathers, Abraham, Isaac, and Jacob"... a God of three generations. Even as God keeps His focus on the "Big Picture" we too must also remember to keep our focus on the "Big Picture"... a vision of at least three generations.

Next we must understand how a **behavior system or scheme** begins. In Revelation 3:15-17,20 to the church at Laodicea Jesus says, "I know your deeds, that you are neither cold nor hot; I would that you were cold or hot, So because you are lukewarm, and neither hot nor cold, I will spit you out of my mouth. Because you say, 'I am rich and have become wealthy, and have *need of nothing*... Behold, I stand at the door and knock; if anyone hears my voice and opens the door, I will come in to him and will dine with him, and he with me."

So it is with the church of this day, a church that is not so aware of her *needs*. The apostle Paul speaks of these *needs* saying, "And my God shall supply all your *needs* according to His riches in glory in Christ Jesus." (Philippians 4:19)

The word "supply" in the Greek is the word "plaroo" which means, "to fill." With what does God *fill our needs*? He fills them with "His riches in glory." "Glory" literally is His "tangible relational presence!" Each *need* we have in our life is an opportunity to experience the "tangible relational presence" of God!

Yet two things are sure from these verses we have read:

1. We have legitimate needs.
2. God will supply our needs by means of His glory (tangible relational presence).

Remember, though, that the primary characteristic of the church at Laodicea was that they did not recognize their *need*. What is the deepest *need* that consumes your thoughts and occupies your time? Each of us has a legitimate need to be loved, a legitimate need to be approved, and a legitimate need of contentment and fulfillment.

The first issue we face is that of ***admitting our need***. Our society shuns "need" as weakness, yet God designed needs to be the cause in our lives that motivates us towards Him. The destructive behavior system is supported and developed by four aspects of our value system:

1. **We judge ourselves by our values** that support our behavior system, thus justifying our worth and significance.

For example, it is very common among professional athletes to have their identity anchored in their athletic ability. They will have a set of standards that they can achieve, thus deriving their sense of value and worth. They will always judge themselves by these standards, thus producing a driven person.

2. **Usually these values build up a wall by which we attempt to protect a particular area of expertise**, so that no other can get close. This is a means of protecting an area of weakness, which hold us in bondage to the fear of shame. Frequently this is a hidden sin, habit, or dream, which no one else knows about.

For example, a minister, that upon understanding this truth came to the realization that he had quarantined off the area of spiritual things. He was a spiritual man and gained his worth and significance from his "spirituality". His worth was *relative* rather than *intrinsic* therefore subject to extreme highs and lows.

The result was in order to protect himself he did not help press his wife into spiritual things. In fact, the converse was true. She wanted to get up early to spend time with the Lord, so he would just "forget" to wake her up. The motivation behind this failure was to guard his identity . . . his value and uniqueness of being spiritual. So behind this wall of values lies an ugly heart. It may feel fine, but if left in this lie, will soon move into self-deception.

3. **We begin to judge others by our values**, this way insuring the ongoing of our worth. However, what happens if someone happens to meet our particular set of values? We then make them an idol!

For example, among professional golfers, Tiger Woods is the idol. He is the one who has been able to achieve the extremely high standards that other professional golfers have set. Therefore, now it is commonplace at PGA tournaments to see bodyguards and media personnel following each "popular" player.

4. **We judge God**. By the very fact that we have a value other than the presence of Jesus says to God, "You lied! You will not meet my needs!" Disappointing circumstances sow into our hearts the idea that God will not meet our needs. Without conscious interruption and correction, this idea will lie under the surface of our conscious thought, always provoking our own efforts.

Therefore, with these four props holding up our behavior system, we next need to understand how the behavior system gets in place in our lives. So lets begin with the author of the destructive behavior systems.... the devil.

Is the devil powerless?

Hebrews 2:14-15 says, "Since then the children share in flesh and blood, He Himself likewise also partook of the same, that through death He might render powerless him who had the power of death, that is, the devil; (15) and might deliver those who through fear of death were subject to slavery all their lives." After a quick reading of this passage, we need to consider one particular question. According

Issues

---

to this passage, does the devil have power? Perhaps more appropriately asked, how does the devil get his power?

There are a finite (limited) number of demons. Simply stated, demons don't get together and make baby demons. With this important fact in mind, also note that we in within the Kingdom of God are an ever-growing number. So how does the enemy handle this problem? Two special verses are notes:

- Ephesians 6:11 says "Put on the full armor of God that you may be able to stand firm against the *schemes* of the devil."
- 2 Corinthians 2:11 says, "Do not be ignorant concerning the schemes of the enemy."

A scheme is ***a web or network of iniquities designed to extract your power.*** Remember 1John 2 says, "that you have an anointing." This anointing is the source of your power.

It begins with a lie. The ultimate purpose of the enemy is to get you to ***disconnect your faith***. The enemy whispers a *lie* to get you to push away your faith. Because in the absence of faith, ***iniquities*** find expression and you get ***offended***. (See chapter 10 – "Offended!")

- Remember, you can't get offended when you are in faith. 1 Peter 2:7, 8 "… but for those who disbelieve … the stone which the builders rejected…became a stone of stumbling and a rock of offense; for they stumble because they are disobedient to the word…".
- With each ***offence**,* you ***leak*** your anointing … the enemy extracts some of your power.

Iniquities Root to a Behavior System – Iniquities are like a seed blowing in the wind, until they find a root. Proverbs 26:2 says, "without a cause a curse does not alight." So there are five basic roots that ground the *behavior system*:

In the early stages of our counseling ministry, people would come in because they had noticed a deficiency in their ***behavior***. The counseling session would begin with finding the bondage, then locating the ***root*** of the problem. Once the ***root*** was found "the axe" was laid to the *root* and the *behavior system* is interrupted. There would normally be tremendous deliverance session at this stage of ministry... *but it all seemed to be temporary.*

There are Five Basic Sources or Roots of Destructive Behavior Systems

1. Trans-generational Iniquity - Exodus 20:5 speaks of "visiting the iniquity of the fathers on the children and on the grandchildren to the third and fourth generations." This speaks of the iniquity (the "desire" or "propensity" of sin) passed down from the parent to the child. However, for the iniquity to find expression the individual has to cooperate with the iniquity. This iniquity is passed in the form of a type of *spiritual genetic code.*

2. Repeated Sin - The moment our will is set to cooperate with the iniquity in our heart, "transgression" occurs. "Transgression" is the ***choosing*** to cooperate with the desire of sin. The only thing left is the activity of sin. The inevitable question is, "How many times can you sin before a destructive behavior system sets in?" We don't know, but the safe position is to discontinue the activity of sin.

3. Judgments - Matthew 7:1-2 says, "Judge not lest you are judged; for the manner that you judge, it will be measured out unto you." *Judgment* is like a boomerang, which destines us to be the recipient of our own judgment. Many of us are held in a pattern of destructive behavior because of a *judgment* we have made on someone like our mother or father, without conscious awareness that the judgment is the source of our problem.

Judgments have two "step-children": Vows and Curses. A *vow* is an ***inward determination*** by the mind, will and emotions, against the will and word of God. It may or may not find verbal expression. The sister to the vow is the *curse*. The *curse* is ***an outward verbal expression*** against the will and word of God. It may be spoken upon one's self or most frequently upon others.

4. Soul-ties - This term "*soul-tie*" is a term, which gained popularity and recognition through the special covenant that David had

Issues

with Jonathan. It says of these men that their "souls were tied" one to the other (1Sam.18: 1).

"Soul-ties" are not necessarily a bad thing. Many of us when we enter into marriage desire to find our "soul-mate"... the one whom our soul is forever knitted to... the one with whom we share the deepest secrets of our hearts. Only the most special of relationships is given to this state.

What is a "soul-tie"? It is ***a natural sense that triggers an old behavior pattern or feeling, thought or decision pattern.*** Is there a special song that triggers a special feeling within you? Is there a particular perfume that triggers a nostalgic feeling within you? These are forms of *soul-ties*. So each ***area of our soul has the potential to be tied to a person, place or event ...* and triggered by one of our senses: feel, sight, hearing, taste, and smell**. Soul-ties can be one-sided as well as mutual.

5. Wounds - Technically the wound is not a source, but rather a current expression of the already existing entrenched destructive behavior. If the wound is traumatic enough it must be dealt with before uncovering the other sources of entrenched destructive behavior in the individual. While the wound is not a "source" of entrenched destructive behavior, wounds keep root alive.

Building the Map

Normal counseling **starts** with the noting of the symptoms of the *behavior system*. The **second** step is the *history inventory* that is used to discover patterns within the *behavior system*. These patterns hint towards or indicate the *roots*.

A **third** step in the counseling process is to discover the basic *Lie* that was received (see pg.22). These *Lies* are foundational to the removal of faith. Only in the absence of *faith* can *iniquities* find expression. When a *Lie* is received, a *False Identity* is developed.

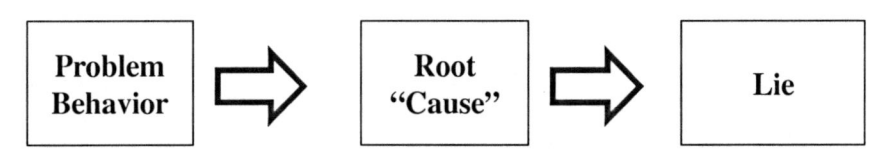

| Problem Behavior | ⇨ | Root "Cause" | ⇨ | Lie |

In Genesis 3, we have the record of the fall of man. This account unfolds the truths of man's struggle for *Identity* (uniqueness and worth). Prior to the "fall," Genesis 1:26 says that man was made in the *image* and *likeness* of God. Just as God covered each thing He created (i.e. birds have feathers, animals have fur, etc.), man being in the image of God was covered in the *glory* of God. An important truth to remember about **identity** is that *you obtain you identity from your covering*. So man was identified with God. He was their God and they were His people.

Genesis 3 records that man fell and lost his covering. Romans 3:23 says "All have sinned and fall short of the glory of God." Therefore, when man fell, he lost his covering thus losing his identity. Adam attempted to cover himself with *"fig-leaves"*, a type of *false* covering. However, if your identity is derived from covering and your covering is *false*, you are left with a *false identity*!

Now God comes along and finds Adam hiding (which is what man does when his **identity** is wrong... he hides from the presence of God). In addition, God clothes Adam in the body and blood of another, a type of the Lord Jesus. Now the question is, what happened to the *fig leaves*? The scriptures do not emphatically state what happened, but what is suggested is nothing. They were left right where they were. The false covering and the false identity were left in place and God simply covered them with the body and blood of Jesus.

The new covering restored Adam's identity before God, but the old fig leaves hindered his experience of that restored identity. It is the same for us. Unless we remove the old fig leaves, our experience of a restored identity is hindered. For example, when we are born again we are made "more than a conqueror" in Christ, yet the question comes up, "Why do we not experience that identity consistently?" Why do failures riddle our lives if we are "more than conquerors?" The answer is because of old fig leaves that need to be removed.

> *Roots anchor the behavior systems... that produce a false identity*

Behind every *destructive behavior* there is a *false identity* and behind every *false identity (or fig leaf)* is a *scheme or system* designed to perpetuate the *false identity*. This *scheme* is a type of fleshly *system* of activity or thought-life, used to produce, support and protect the *false identity*. The ultimate destination of the scheme is to extract your power.

Schemes or **systems** housed within the ingenuity of the heart using the mind, will and emotions to gain much needed **uniqueness** and **worth**. However, this **uniqueness** and **worth** will be based on the individuals own **value system**. This **value system** defines one's **uniqueness** and **worth**.

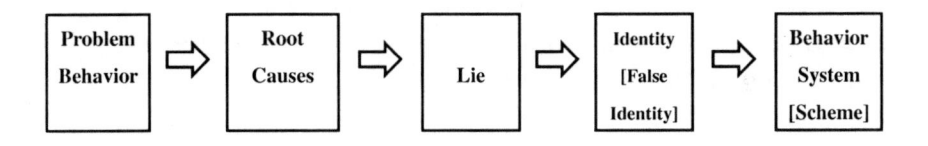

Problem Behavior	⇨	Root Causes	⇨	Lie	⇨	Identity [False Identity]	⇨	Behavior System [Scheme]

Values and Standards

Behind every *fig-leaf* there are *values* and *standards*. *A value system* simply defines *importance*. Values are most clearly seen in the **standards** held by the individual. *Standards are specific, measurable rules designed to reinforce the False Identity*. Standards are determined by the value system. The individual can ultimately achieve their goal of significance and worth under those standards. If the individual fails with a particular set of standards, then the standards are adjusted until they are achievable. [Note *"soul mapping"* on Appendix vi, vii]

The final part to the *"soul mapping"* is the stage of "Bondage" (a biblical term) or dysfunction and super-imposition. *"Dysfunction"* is when *Behavior no longer requires the decision making process, but has evolved into a subconscious action*… it happens without a thought process. Frequently this stage is one that goes beyond the *will*, and functions against some desires. This stage is also characterized by the "super imposition" against the will.

Examples of Schemes

To clarify let's look at some examples of some schemes. First, we will look at a scheme of *perversion*. Let's consider a man whose *identity* is connected to his idea of being a man. In his youth, he was told that real men had to excel in their sexual performance. Both his father and grandfather struggled with infidelity. He has an *iniquity* of wrong sexual desire. He has received a *lie* that he cannot really be a man without certain sexual prowess. However, he is a Christian, perhaps even a pastor, and he fears fulfilling his desires by actual experiences.

His *scheme* is to look at pornography on the internet late at night. He tells his wife that he needs to stay up to study, actually he is looking at pornography on the internet to fulfill the lustful desire within. Do you see the *destructive system*? He tells himself that he isn't doing anything wrong be cause he isn't acting out what he feels with real life experiences, only in fantasy. As long as he continues to watch pornographic movies, he will never be free from perversion, even if he finds the roots and breaks them. He is still feeding a destructive behavior pattern with perversion.

Let's look at an example that is more difficult to discern. An elder in a church is responsible for a large youth ministry. He has workers to help him, but he finds that his schedule is always being disrupted leaving him doing more of the work than he should be doing. Part of his *identity* is that of being a "keeper of the peace". He feels that he is responsible to make everything work out and keep peace in the church. When other needs arise in other areas of the church, he allows people from his team to meet those needs leaving him to handle his area with fewer people.

His value system tells him that he is better equipped to handle such problems than anyone else is. The devil sees to it that plenty of situations arise to take his support team, so he often gets the opportunity to show that he can carry the load and keep things going. He is always tired. He suffers, his family suffers and the youth ministry suffers. This suffering is simply because this leader is trying to be "all things to all people." God wants him to do his job and the others to do theirs. God wants everyone to be dependent on Him.

In counseling ministry, *"soul mapping"* can be most beneficial. Counselors can memorize the chart and then as they listen, can fill in the appropriate *behavior, roots, lies, behavior systems, false identities, values & standards* (visible part of value system). This process of *"soul mapping"* enables us to process the *"cause"* and *"effect"* of the *dysfunctional behavior.* This is one of the primary tools of Christ-O-Therapy.

Mapping

(Steps in Counseling Ministry)

Our protocol to counseling is *First – Education...* help them understand their destructive behavior and how it developed. Understand the *lie* is an important step. *Secondly – Impartation...* gives them help through spiritual reality...(New Birth, deliverance, inner healing, etc.) *Thirdly – Activation...* aids them in walking out the new behavior. This may include discipline aids such as accountability partners and group therapy, renewing the mind, developing boundaries, etc.

1. **Connection Period** – This is the "acquaintance" period where you get to know them.
   - **Empathetic Listening** - Remember, "They have to know how much you care, before they care how much you know."
   - Let them tell their story
   - Keep eye contact
   - Ask questions of interest & clarification
2. **Triage** – "stop the bleeding"
   - **Danger Zones** – physical danger like abuse; emotional trauma's, grief, self-injury, etc.
   - **Need to Stabilize –**
   - **Deal with immediate crisis situations**
   - **Give at least one step of practical activation/implementation.** The purpose of this step is two-fold: to give immediate

"stop-gap" solutions; and to divert the internal emotional energy to external actions.
3. **Set next appointment within 24 hrs.**
4. **Take History**
   - **Natural** – many need a physical (medical exam) – note hereditary problems with dad, mom, siblings, etc.
   - **Spiritual** –
     o **Pre-counseling Inventory** (beginning point)
     o **Listen for patterns of behavior**
     o **Laser Inventory** – targeted questions aimed at gathering insight to a pre-determined suspected area of problem.

     For Example – Couple comes in with "anger" problem: **Questions might be:**
     - When did you first recognize or remember anger explosions?
     - Was anger part of your growing up experience?
     - Pain-Anger Questions: (a) Rejection/ Abuse/ Abandonment/etc.
     - How did that make you feel?

5. **Identify the Roots** – using a history profile inventory, you can search for various patterns of behavior. These patterns of behavior will disclose possible roots. Critical relationships, i.e. father, mother, spouse, etc., will also need to be inventoried to discover possible roots.
6. **Identify the Lie** – behind each root there is a general lie that operates (remember the 3 lies from "Soul Mapping, part I – pg.27-28) After discovering the lie, replace it with truth. A process of "renewing the mind" is necessary for a complete paradigm change, especially as it pertains to changing from the **False Identity** to a **Legitimate Identity**.
7. **Identify Value sources & Identity wounds** - from where do you get your sense of value, worth, significance, belonging? These areas of wounding seem to present the most difficult of problems.

8. **False Identity (Fig Leaf)** - Expose the False Identity.
   - Confess lie which produces the wrong identity
   - Confess right identity in place
   - **Outline the Values and Standards that support the False Identity.** Interrupt and replace the **values & standards**. Remember that the "value system" has to change in order for the behavior to change on a long-term basis.
9. **Dysfunction – "*Christ-O-Therapy*" is needed to complete the Restoration process.** Besides the already mentioned facets of the Restoration process, some additional aids might include:

   - Accountability – personal accountability may be needed to reinforce the weakened behavior
   - Support Groups – helpful in aiding one in "processing" problems
   - Personal Discipleship/Mentoring – necessary for ongoing growth and personal development.

10. **Healing of heart / Memories / Child within** – this part of "*Christ-O-Therapy*" may involve a type of "prophetic counseling" where "words of knowledge" and "words of wisdom" are instrumental. This type of counseling enables us to go into the past (memory regression) and then bring the emotions forward into the present. This is different from *Recovered Memory Therapy* in that simple *enlightenment* of the past does not bring resolution… only enlightenment, which can actually result in more pain! There is still healing that needs to take place within the emotions. *Complete healing is usually a process* involving memories, relationship deconstruction (offences, abandonment, abuse, etc.), pain resulting from the wounds received (remember wounds are based on perception, not necessarily reality), actual *processing* or *understanding* of the issue, *choice to re-engage* (from a basis of forgiveness), re-attachment, and refocus or redirection. Remember that *wounds keep roots alive.*

Our Ten Core Needs

Diagnostic Questions – What is the greatest need in your life? What do you spend the most of your time thinking about? What steps are you taking to meet this most important need in your life? What will happen if this need is not met?

Prognosis – The needs in our lives are met either through a relationship with God or through our own abilities. Although there may be human channels for meeting those needs, ultimately the source must be God.

Remedy – The key to resolving need-issues is to find that core need met through your relationship God. This "presence" based or "relational" based key is the topic of this chapter.

James 4:1-5 "What is the source of quarrels and conflicts among you? Is not the source your pleasures that wage war in your members?" James says that the source of conflict is the desire for pleasure. We have already spoken about ***iniquity...the desire to sin***. There are three things that seem to work together: *flesh, iniquity* (or desire toward the world's pleasure) and the *demonic*. These three are in concert to lead us into destructive behavior.

In Galatians 5:16-25 the apostle Paul says "But I say, walk by the Spirit, and you will not carry out the desire of the flesh..." There is a war being waged inside us. The desires of the flesh, the desires of this world and the desires of the enemy are against the desires of God. Now what are they waging war over? They are warring for

control of the soul. Why do they want the soul? What is so important about the soul of man? It is the seat of man's mind, will and emotions. Whatever controls the soul controls the man and all that he does. The soul is the "translator" for the spirit... receiving from the spirit, and translating into "sense world" terminology.

God also desires to first connect Himself to us, then through us. The soul is like a radio receiver. It communicates the invisible signal it receives into a sound that communicates with others. In the same way, spiritual things come by the spirit, but it must pass through the soul. The soul will express the character of whatever controls it, be it the flesh or be it God. So, there is a battle taking place for the soul.

God wants His presence to connect to and through you. Why is this important? This is the way God has chosen to release His influence into the world. It is His presence, which brings "light" into the world. The Bible tells us that the ruler of this present world is Satan. He was given delegated authority in this world when Adam sinned and yielded his God-given authority to Satan. He remains in control of this world until a greater authority displaces him.

Jesus came as a superior authority and broke Satan's legal right to rule, but each heart and soul must still be possessed. It will have to be taken by a superior force. That force is God's presence. He has chosen to release His power and authority through men (Genesis 1:26-28). If we release the presence of God through us, it will break the rule and reign of Satan on this earth. We will issue in a new superior authority.

Therefore, the enemy does not want you or I to connect to the presence of God. The results is there is a war over the soul, a war to control the soul. If your soul connects to iniquities, or flesh, or the demonic, it will manifest those things not of the kingdom of God. But when our soul connects with the presence of God, this connection presents a stronger influence than that of the enemy. Our soul must come into agreement with the Spirit of God in our spirit.

What will Satan leverage to capture our souls? There has to be something that *motivates* the soul, and it is within this *motivation* that the devil works. Man's soul is motivated by his *need*. Every man has *legitimate needs* in his life. These needs must be met. His soul will search for a way to meet these needs. Either they will be met by connecting to the presence of God or they'll be met by some other illegitimate source.

The apostle Paul says in Philippians 4:19 "...And my *God shall supply* all your *needs* according to His riches in glory in Christ Jesus." In this incredible verse Paul connects our needs with the (glory) tangible relational presence of God.

Then again in Revelation 3:15-17 the apostle John says, "... because you say, "I am rich, and have become wealthy, and have *need of nothing*, and you do not know that you are wretched and miserable and poor and blind and naked." The church in Laodicea felt like their needs were met, and obviously, Jesus felt they were not. In fact, the church was indicative of many today... those who are not *self-aware.* This posture of *self-awareness* is called... *humility.*

God has formed each of us with *needs*. He wants us to *need* Him and to depend on Him. In our weakness, He becomes strong within us. It is our *needs* that cause us to seek God. But our *needs* can also cause us to seek satisfaction in things other than God. Satan uses our *needs* as leverage to get us to seek their fulfillment in anything but in God. If he can get us to put our hope in anything other than God, he can draw us into dependency on that thing.

In this chapter we are going to get a basic understanding of the fundamental *needs* that God has placed in every human life, to understand how each need is to be rightly met, and to understand the pitfalls of trying to meet those *needs* in wrong ways. When they are wrongly met they bring a *destructive behavior system (bondage).* ***This destructive behavior system is the result of seeking to meet a legitimate need in an illegitimate way.*** When we do not connect to the presence of God to get a *need* met, we put ourselves in position to get into a *pattern of destructive behavior.*

The *needs* that we are referring to are not those needs that will keep our body alive. We aren't talking about our need for air, water or food. The needs we are talking about are those needs that are involved in the battle for the soul, and we find them in the twentieth chapter of Exodus where God gives the *Ten Commandments.* We have looked at the *Ten Commandments* as a list of "don'ts," but they are more than that. Each commandment was set forth to protect a *core need* that God has placed within us. They are divine guardians of *core needs* in our life. If we understand what they are to protect, we can identify the needs that exist.

1. Core Need - Identity

"You shall have no other gods before Me." Exodus 20:3

This commandment guards the need for ***identity.*** A sense of ***identity is a foundational need*** in anyone's life. We must know who we are and where we fit into the scheme of things in this world. When we don't have a sense of being someone and belonging somewhere, we don't have anything. So whatever gives us identity will frequently be the most important thing in our life. This area of identity is most normally developed during the "formative years" in connection with the primary "care-giver" (usually the parents).

The three primary components of Identity are (1) *intrinsic worth*, (2) *relative significance or uniqueness* and (3) a *sense of belonging*.

The component of ***intrinsic worth*** is connected to our "***approval factor.***" This ***approval*** is detected by feelings of ***affirmation, confirmation*** and ***validation***. ***Affirmation*** is the "building up" of the individual. ***Confirmation*** is public affirmation. ***Validation*** is a stamp of authenticity and originality.

This approval is usually communicated verbally. It might sound like "You are fantastic! I am so proud of you! Your are very important to us." When spoken by the primary care-givers, these words create a strong feeling of value and worth.

In addition to the ***approval*** from the primary life-givers, there is an ***approval*** that comes from Father-God. Even Jesus at His baptism modeled this *Father-God approval.* As the Holy Spirit descended in the form of a dove, Father-God spoke over His son, "This is my beloved Son, in whom I greatly approve." These words of affirmation spoken by Father-God, deep into the heart of the individual imparts real feeling of value and worth. So not only through primary care-givers, but also through a vital connection with Father-God, this component of Identity is developed.

The second component of *identity* is that of *relative significance or uniqueness.* While worth and value are intrinsic, significance or uniqueness is relative... by definition requires more than one to feel unique. This component is usually developed by attention and appreciation. By conveying appropriate interest, concern, and care... by entering their world... the primary care-giver imparts a deep sense of special-ness. Each of us are different by intentional design, and our unique design can contribute to our sense of value, or deprive us of this sense of value and special-ness. This impartation of significance is not only given by "entering their world" to show them how important they are, but by also showing appropriate appreciation, praise, or commendation... recognizing their accomplishment and effort. This is usually done verbally with expressions such as, "You did a great job! I appreciate your diligence. You are really working hard."

The third component of *identity* is that of *a sense of belonging.* This is usually accomplished by the primary care-givers within the context of a *family.* A second player in the development of this component of *identity* is that of the *Family of God.* In a society of broken homes, this aspect of *belonging* is key to developing this sense of acceptance. A third aid in developing this aspect of *identity* are other *"family"* oriented groups, *i.e. gangs, clubs, fraternities, etc.* The difficulty with this component is that it requires an unconditional type of acceptance... a type of acceptance that gives the freedom to fail... a type of acceptance that continues caring for another in spite of offences.

When people do not develop a healthy identity and self-esteem during formative years, they will continue to search and draw their identity from all sorts of things. It is frequently based on a type of performance orientation, such as their job, a sport, or their social ability. It is also frequently based on looks or intelligence. It can be based on almost anything. Whatever makes the person *feel they are of value*, needed, or useful usually results in being his identity.

But what happens if a person's identity is in the type of things we mentioned? He can lose his job, or the job that he did so well can be replaced by a machine. Beauty fades with age, and so does physical ability. The only secure place for identity is in something that cannot change or be affected by the world's circumstances. The greatest need of our life is to have our identity anchored by our relationship with Jesus Christ. He is the rock on which the house of our life is to be built. He is the only thing that will stand in the storms of life. That's why God set that protector guardian as a commandment upon that need.

How Do You Connect to the Presence of God for Identity – Exodus 3:10-14

2 Part Anchor

Gods Presence "to you" – In Exodus 3:14 we find the famous phrase "*I Am That I Am.*" This anchor is secured by developing your intimacy with God. Such intimacy will illumine "who you are" by beginning to define who God is to you. Only when you can answer who God is to you is the first anchor secured. In the early chapters of the Bible, God declares that He made man in His image and likeness. Therefore, as we get to know Him, the one we are like, we get to know ourselves.

One day the apostle Peter was confronted by Jesus with the question, "Who do men say that I am?" Before Jesus would take Peter a step further towards his ministry and his destiny, Jesus knew that this area of Identity must be anchored.

Gods Presence "through you" or "through others to you" – In Exodus 3:12 God speaks to Moses and tells him, "Certainly I will be with you." The second anchor is that of a **conscious recognition that it is God who is at work through you**. Not your desires alone, not your dreams alone, but His desires and dreams working through you. It is a conscious awareness of God's presence working through you.

For example, if we are a mother or a father, our responsibility is not to simply be a mother or father, but is to allow the Lord to express Himself as a mother or father through us. If I am a teacher by profession, my identity is not to be a teacher, but to allow the Lord to teach through me. It is not to be simply a wife or husband, but to allow the Lord to meet our wife's or husband's needs through us. Because we are created uniquely, we will express some parts of His character differently than others, and we will express them in the way that only our character can. Our expression will not be like yours. But we will both be expressing God's nature and life. So when we are aware of a need, we look to the Lord to see if He desires to meet the need for us or through us. In this way He is responsible for the results.

Who are we? We are wonderfully unique creations of God. Each of us is designed with a particular purpose, created to make a difference. Finding our significance in our relationship with Jesus will set us free from trying to be something or someone we are not.

2. Core Need - Reality

"You shall not make for yourself an idol..." Exodus 20:4

As a child, I was a best friend with a Catholic girl. Being from an evangelical home, I was very unfamiliar with the customs and traditions of the Catholic religion. The part that always intrigued me was the little medallion that was worn around the neck and the little statue that was on the dash of their automobiles. When I inquired about them, I was informed that they were Saints that would protect them. A little later, I asked the pastor of the church we attended and he told me they were *idols.*

I later learned that *idols* were simply **anything that replaces the real or true; thus, that which is false.** So in this sense there are many things besides statues that qualify as idols in this day. The primary word in each of Webster's definition of idolatry is the word *excess*. So anything in *excess* has the potential to become *idolatry* and *detach us from reality*. For example, the love of a parent to a child, as good and natural as it is, has the potential to become *idolatry* when found in *excess*.

A special note is found in Exodus 20:4, to not make an "idol" or in other translations, "a graven image ...or any likeness." It's important to read this verse alongside of Genesis 1:26 when God says, "let Us make man in Our image and likeness." The word *image* means literally the *imprint*. While the word *likeness* denotes the *activity* of the *imprint*. Therefore, the reference to an idol is not only the *image* of that idol (or excess) but also rather, *the activity* of that same idol.

So amidst our incredible need for reality and life, God sets this protector. Many things detract and detour us from *reality*... from that which brings life, and they become **substitutes** for life itself. Have you ever known one who has fallen away from God, then tried to come back to God? They began to do all the things, rituals, and disciplines they did formerly. They put their Bible beside their bed; they get up early and read the bible – pray one hour – or whatever brought them life formerly ... thinking that in these forms they would re-connect with reality and life. It is when these substitutes for Life are interrupted or violated that difficulty occurs.

Therefore, problems occur when the **Need for Reality** is being met in an illegitimate way. *Illegitimacy* is the state where there is no presence of God. Instead, we find form and boundaries rather than freedom and liberty. We also find past & future words from God rather than present words. People act like slaves rather than sons... where people are in the image, but not the likeness of God. Finally, it is a place where faith has come to people, but they have not come to faith. Any of these substitutes for *reality*, when depended upon for *reality,* can create *destructive behavior patterns*.

When we feel insecure or our self-esteem is low, there is a tendency to escape from reality. We escape through many different ways. Sometimes we medicate the pain. Other times we escape through fantasy... movies, television, etc. All of us need periods of rest. But when the rest turns into escape... and continues on a daily basis, the tendency is to disconnect from reality. This disconnection from reality, when supported by repetition, can become a destructive behavior.

I received a call from Lisa. She wanted an appointment to discuss her relationship with her husband. When she arrived, she was seated in my office while I finished a telephone call in another room. When I entered the room, after a normal greeting, the first words out of her mouth were, "could we begin with prayer?" I responded with a simply, "of course." Before I could open my mouth to pray, she began what turned into a fifteen-minute oratory about the family.

When she concluded I said a loud, "Amen." Then I turned my gaze towards her and asked the most dangerous of counseling questions, "What is the problem?"

She then began to tell me how her husband was not spiritual. How he did not pray enough…read his Bible enough…watched too much television…did not really hear God. After about twenty minutes of listening to the story, I interrupted with a question. "Lisa, would you describe your last encounter with God?" Her answer was scrambled with religious terms that even I after 25 years of ministry, had difficulty interpreting. Lisa looked at me for a nod of approval… but my silence told her the truth. As tears began to well in her eyes, I said, "Lisa, tell me in non-religious terms about your most recent encounter with God." She simply hung her head in silence, as she began to cry.

Reality had gone… religion had taken its place. Problems were rising on every horizon of her life, especially her marriage. The more intimate the relationship, the more difficult the problems… because of the absence of Reality. The connection with the Presence of God is gone… this is reality... and the more intimate the relationship, the greater the tendency to "disconnect". Finally after what seemed to be a lifetime, I said to Lisa, "Lisa, spirituality without reality is only mysticism." She looked at me with tears still flowing, and nodded. I asked her if I could pray for her, and she agreed. I then began to pray for God to remove the false and replace it with the Real. By the time I had finished, the tear washed face glowed with a new touch of the Presence of the Lord. We had once again connected with *reality*.

3. Core Need – To Make Decisions

"You shall not take the name of the Lord your God in vain."
Exodus 20:7

The first command that God gave man was to "be fruitful and multiply, replenish… subdue… and rule!" God created man to rule and to exercise authority. The problem is the manner in which this "ruling" or "exercising of Authority" is being handled. One of the most prevalent destructive behavior systems is a crippling problem known as "codependency." The basic nature of "codependency" is that one is rendered dysfunctional due to the lack of making his/her own decisions…thus they are found to be dependant on others for this service.

Codependency is usually the result of one of two types of environments: (1) a Controlling environment – the freedom of choice is taken (usually called domination) (2) a Lawless or defaulting environment.

One of many definitions of codependency is: "a set of *maladaptive, *compulsive behaviors learned by family members in order to survive in a family which is experiencing *great emotional pain and stress."

****maladaptive*** - inability for a person to develop behaviors which get needs met.
****compulsive*** – a psychological state where a person acts against their own will or conscious desires.
*****sources of great emotional pain and stress** - chemical dependency; chronic mental illness; chronic physical illness; physical abuse; sexual abuse; emotional abuse; divorce; hypercritical or non-loving environment.

As adults, codependent people have a greater tendency to get involved in relationships with people who are perhaps unreliable, emotionally unavailable, or needy. And the codependent person tries to provide and control everything within the relationship without addressing their own needs or desires; setting themselves up for continued unfulfillment. Desires for **approval** and **validation** are usually at the center of a codependent person. Therefore, when one finds someone who will validate them and give approval to them, they relinquish their identity, their right to have opinion and individuality (uniqueness) to that person.

Even when a codependent person encounters someone with healthy boundaries, the codependent person still operates in their own system; they're not likely to get too involved with people who have healthy boundaries. This of course creates problems that continue to recycle; if codependent people can't get involved with people who have healthy behaviors and coping skills, then the problems continue into each new relationship.

How do I know if I'm codependent?

Generally, if you're feeling unfulfilled consistently in relationships, you tend to be indirect, don't assert yourself when you have a need, if you're able to recognize you don't play as much as others, or other people point out you could be more playful. Things like this can indicate you're codependent.

What are some of the symptoms?

* controlling behavior
* distrust
* perfectionism
* avoidance of feelings
* intimacy problems
* caretaking behavior
* hyper-vigilance (a heightened awareness for potential threat/danger)
* physical illness related to stress

Isn't everyone codependent?

There are some natural and healthy behaviors mothers do with children that look like codependency. Are people mutually interdependent on each other? Yes. There is perhaps a continuum of codependency, that most people might fall on. Maybe this continuum exists because so many people are taught not to be assertive, or to ask directly for their needs to be met? We probably can't say though that everyone is codependent. Many people probably don't feel fulfilled because of other things going on in the system at large.

Why do we become codependent? What causes it?

It's widely believed we become codependent through living in systems (families) with rules that hinder development to some degree. The system (usually parents and relatives) has been developed in response to some problem such as alcoholism, mental illness or some other *secret or problem*.

General rules set-up within families that may cause codependency may include:

* It's not okay to talk about problems
* Feelings should not be expressed openly; keep feelings to yourself
* Communication is best if indirect; one person acts as messenger between two others; known in therapy as triangulation
* Be strong, good, right, perfect
* Make us proud beyond realistic expectations
* Don't be selfish
* Do as I say not as I do
* It's not okay to play or be playful
* Don't rock the boat.

Many families have one or more of these rules in place within the family. These kinds of rules can constrict and strain the free and healthy development of people's self-esteem, and coping. As a result, children can develop non-helpful behavior characteristics, problems solving techniques, and reactions to situations in adult life

4. Core Need – To Trust

"Remember the Sabbath day, to keep it holy." Exodus 20:8

This commandment guards the legitimate need *to trust*. The word "Sabbath" means to "repose, to desist from exertion; to cease, to rest." Isaiah 58:13-14 tells us that the provision and blessing of the Lord are directly related to keeping the Sabbath. Fruitfulness is directly related to keeping the Sabbath.

The Sabbath was consistently taught and applied to the lives of God's people, from Adam to Noah to Abraham to the people of Israel. Hebrews 4:1-11 applies the principle of the Sabbath rest to those of us in the new covenant. When Israel failed to enter Canaan it was said that it was due to their **unbelief. "Belief" or "unbelief"** is the **activity of faith, which** *is begun through the decision of trust.* When we are obedient to the voice of God in our lives, we can *trust* God for the results therefore, we can be at *rest*. However, when we do not know that we have been obedient or that we have heard God, we cannot rest. Additionally, if **because of wounds in our hearts, we are unable to trust** God with the results, we cannot rest. Instead, we enter into **performance** to bring about results by the power of our own works. This results in striving and anxiety, and it robs us of the rest God intended. So begin to see that *rest* **is connected to** *trust*.

It is important to see and understand that within the process of wounding, that trust is frequently disconnected, and even sometimes completely destroyed. So critical is this *trust* issue, that in the Old Testament, along with the "guilt offering" there was another offering called "restitution" offering. The very purpose of this offering was to initiate the **re-connection** of trust.

Two Ingredients to Disconnected Trust

There are two ingredients to a disconnected trust relationship:

(1) The **type of violation** (lie, deceit, cheating, infidelity, etc)
(2) The **level of the relationship violated** (friend, partner, spouse, etc) It can be as mild as a small lie your neighbor told you ... to an infidelity within a marriage relationship.

So, Why Trust?

The most common ways we react to people who are hurting fall basically into two categories:.. **moralistic** and **psychological**. The moralist approach looks for "cause and effect" within a set of morals... for the Christian, we look to the Bible to define those morals. This approach then requires a change of mind and a change of behavior usually through a "choice" process. By choosing to embrace certain principles and truths, and choosing to embrace change, we adapt a different behavior.

The **psychological approach** tries to find out what is wrong internally, and then helps us learn healthier more productive ways of living. This process often takes months of self-exploration to find the roots of our problem, and to chart a course towards self-awareness and better ways of coping with the issues.

I believe that there is a third approach. Could it be, that God has put within each of us His power, which, when we **connect** with another person, allows us to find the good that God has already put in them, and to release that good so that they can respond to the good urges God has placed there?

This is the main premise **(1) "The center of a forgiven person is not sin. Neither is it psychological complexity. The center of a person is the capacity to connect."(2) The gift of salvation gives us the Holy Spirit, Who allows us first to connect with God the Father, and then, on a new and deeper level, with each other.** But what is connecting?

Look at the Trinity. The Trinity, "an Eternal Community **of three fully connected persons."(3) They have delighted in each other for eternity, there is no shadow of envy or minute bit of jealousy between them, and they love to do what is best for each other.** Since God made us in His image, we too can enjoy one another, but we must rely on the power of God in us to show us what is good in the other person.

Connecting is so powerful because it requires that we look past the surface of people and see their divine potential. Connecting with someone else requires us to look at what a person could be, not just what he is right now. With God's insight, we look beyond the small amount God may already have done and ask God for a vision of what this person could be like. **Connecting finds the spark in someone else and is excited about what it could flame into.**

So how do we develop trust? How do we reconnect broken trust? There are three stages to the growth of trust:

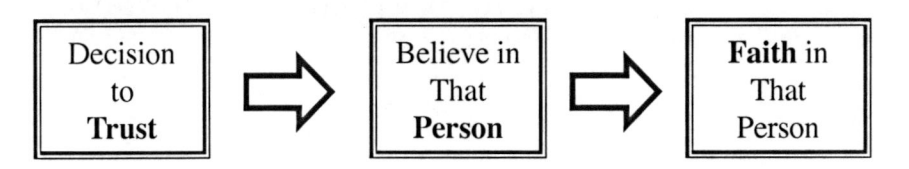

| Decision to **Trust** | ⇒ | Believe in That **Person** | ⇒ | **Faith** in That Person |

Trust is a decision. It is the doorway to belief, which is the activity of faith. But what type of person do you trust? Did you know that there are certain character traits that endear trust? Let me profile a Trustworthy person for you:

<u>*Attributes that Endear Trust*</u>
- Morality absolutes (honest)
- Self esteem (lack of need orientation)
- Empathetic
- Level of Disclosure (transparency)
- Able to accept criticism
- Forgiving

<u>*Attributes that Dissuade Trust*</u>
- Guarded (not transparent)
- Need Driven
- A-moral (not completely honest)
- Restricted Feelings
- Judgmental, Critical
- Resentful
- Competitive
- Track record of distrust

Once a **decision to trust** is made (usually from a type of discernment or assessment using both intuition and observation), that decision grows into belief through **reinforcement repetition**. Repeated experiences of trust and honesty, forgiveness and empathy, reinforce the decision and activate your believing. **Everyone needs someone to believe in them.** Finally the last stage is that **of Faith in them**

as a person. No longer is it a growing process, but now the line has been crossed and **resolve** is in place. No more tests and events of reinforcement are necessary. You have **placed faith** in that person.

Now comes the inevitable question: What do you do when your trust is betrayed... you are lied to, you are cheated, you are betrayed... now what?

Remember, the fabric of relationships is the fabric of trust. So **the foundation of ongoing trust is the ability to forgive.** Remember the **six keys to complete forgiveness**.

- Forgiveness is a Choice, not a feeling
- We don't forgive because they are worth it – we forgive because He asked us to forgive
- We do not forgive out of our own resources, but from the mercy He has given us
- We must release expectations / rights (Mt.18:27)
- Hebrews 10:18 says, "where there is forgiveness, there no longer remains any offering for sin." The word "offering" literally means "a price to be paid; something to be done." So when you say to someone, "I forgive you" you are releasing him or her from any further responsibility of response.
- Where necessary, forgive yourself.

Once forgiveness is in place, you need **to allow healing to take place**. But healing must take place in a "safe environment" or a "safe place." The key to this "safe place" is the proper use of "boundaries." [We have included a brief article on the proper use of boundaries in your syllabus] \

Now, it is imperative that this healing take place so that you can reconnect your heart to the one forgiven. This healing is most frequently achieved through others. Healing is a "body" activity... therefore must be achieved through the hands of others. Many times a counselor or pastor is helpful with this step. For the past couple of decades the term "inner healing" has become popular. This term describes the process of healing the heart so that it can reconnect.

Reconnection is one of the most difficult, but important steps. Before I speak to you about **reconnection**, I want to share with you that there are four distinct personality types that have difficulty with this stage of **reconnection. Remember,** your ability to trust is dominantly formed during you adolescent & formative years. Remember that Proverbs speaks of learning trust upon your mother's breast.

1. Controllers – these are the type that are self aware… they know their strengths, and have solid sense of their adequacy to meet whatever lies ahead. Controllers depend on their own resources to bring a sense of control into their lives. Their adequacy, which is self-derived, blocks them from depending on God.

2. Destiny Determiners – are people to must have a plan they know will work. Due to life's issues, this person has become the ultimate pragmatist. They hold close to their plans and trust their plans, so connecting is hard for them because it would require them to trust God and not know what might happen next.

3. Fearful Protectors – due to events of life, many times during their formative years, they build walls to protect themselves and their families from their fears. Their lives are in such a "protective" mode, they are unable to engage trust. Frequently tragedies in life cause us to slip into the ultra protective mode. Frequently being raised in a place that feels "unsafe" will produce the "fearful protector" syndrome.

4. Wanting Wanderer – this individual is seeking contentment and fulfillment. We want to be fulfilled and we want it immediately. We live in a fast-everything world…a microwave society. We wonder why God is taking so long to bring along the right woman or man, so we find our own ways to satisfy our desires, whether in pornography, or cheap sex, or relationships we know can't last.

No matter what type of personality we have, we have to deal with the issues that support these dysfunctional personalities so that we can connect to others.

Reconnection involves several steps:

- Reconnection is only possible from the **foundation of forgiveness**...
- We reconnect our trust in a Big God... who is able to "turn the hearts of kings wherever He wishes." This step **focuses on the ability of God** rather than the trustworthiness of man. We look through the man to the ability and faithfulness of God.
- We process the wound **mentally**. We try to understand why it happened & the effects of the wounds. Frequently a counselor and trusted friend can help with this step. A skilled counselor can aid you in discovering cause and effect. A friend can provide emotional support.
- We process the wound **volitionally**. We choose to forgive, we choose to break judgments, we choose to receive healing, we choose to trust again.
- We process the wound **emotionally**. This is where we receive healing vicariously through others. If forgiveness is not in place, we will have confusing feelings of vengeance & retribution.
- **Boundaries** must be set in place to insure a "safe place" for healing and reconnection.
- **Reinforcement** by repetition of experience activates our "believing"
- "**Faith**" is reinstated

5. Core Need – To be Accountable

"Honor your father and your mother..." Exodus 20:12

This commandment guards man's need to *be Accountable*. *This is the balance to having authority*. It includes both "accountability" and "responsibility" towards others. Remember in the eighth chapter of Matthew that Jesus marveled at the centurion because he understood the need to be under authority. This "accountability" or "responsibility" are more than a position, it is an attitude of heart (honor). *No one has authority to any greater extent than they are under authority.* The authority over us is our covering, our protection. It gives us security. Those who reject authority manifest lawlessness, rebellion and pride. They don't trust anyone. They are always forced to protect themselves. They live in fear.

It is interesting that of all the commandments, this is the only one with a "promise." Remember that the promise is one of "long life" and "well being" or "health." A practical application of this principle might be to develop your own "Inner Circle" (a term taken from John Maxwell's "21 Irrefutable Laws of Leadership"). This group consists of two or three trusted friends that you give the right to "get in your face" as well as support you. Your commitment to them is to be *honest* and *transparent*. Their commitment to you is *to love you* and to *hold confidence*.

When this core need is not being meet there will be feeling of fear and harm. When this core need is being met there will be a sense of dependability... keeping of promises... providing appropriate limits and reasonably enforcing them. When this core need is being met there will be words spoken like "I am here for you. We're going to work this out. I'm going to keep my promise to you."

6. Core Need – To Love & be loved

"You shall not murder." Exodus 20:13

Murder or killing is the ultimate activity of hatred. Jesus taught in the Sermon on the Mount in Matthew 5:21-26 that if you have hated, and then you have murdered in your heart. This commandment guards man's legitimate need to be loved and accepted. Rejection is the ultimate wound that causes hatred to rise up in a man. We all need to be loved and accepted by somebody.

When a person perceives that he is not being loved, there are three wrong responses that are possible.

- The first is the **Mirror Response** - he becomes angry and answers rejection with rejection.

- The second response is **Transference**. He may withdraw his love from the person from whom he was looking for love and transfer it to someone else. This happens many times in a divorce situation. A divorcee transfers his or her love to the children. Another example might be a young woman who isn't receiving the love she needs within her family. She may get pregnant and transfer all her love to the baby. A baby can't reject her.
- A third response is **Withdrawal**. The person vows to never love again. He builds walls around his heart and won't let anyone in.

None of these wrong responses satisfy the need for love. They all drive the person deeper into rejection. There is **a right way** for meeting our need for love. The opposite of this is *acceptance* which is the *receiving another person willingly and unconditionally, especially when the other's behavior has been imperfect. Being willing to continue caring for another in spite of offences.* This core need gives another the freedom to fail; the giving of another chance. You will hear words like, *"I know that you want to do better. I'm looking forward to working together on this problem."*

Right Responses to Rejection

1. Receive God's love for you. 1John 4:19 says, "We love because He first loved us." Draw your need for love through your relationship with Jesus. You can't give love to another without trying to draw your own need from that person unless you first get your need met from the Lord.

2. We have to love ourselves to be able to love others. Galatians 5:14 "...You shall love your neighbor *as* yourself." This shows that we cannot love our neighbor unless we first love ourselves. We have to accept ourselves.

Five Basic Hindrances to Loving One's Self

1. **Shame over past failures** - we must receive forgiveness.

2. **Shame of the present** - this means we are living in pretense and trying to hide sin. We will have to confess the sin and repent. **Two Types of Shame:** (1) Shame, which emanates from what you have done (2) Shame which emanates from what others have said about you.

3. **Received lies about ourselves** – these lies are most frequently given us through other people. We must choose to believe who the Bible says we are. Meditate on that and set our mind and heart to believe what the Bible says as opposed to what people have said. Ask the Holy Spirit to bring to life the revelation of who we are in Jesus.

4. **Angry at God** – the feel that God let them down and they don't know who to blame.

5. **Lack of Purpose** – many times shame hides your purpose. Confused by the feelings of unworthiness, one fails to discover their true destiny.

Seek to put all wrong relationships right. Release all bitterness and judgment toward other people, starting with our immediate family. Forgive offenses that we have received, and ask for forgiveness for offenses that we have given. Release other people from our expectations, and place our hope in the faithfulness of God, not in other people.

7. Core Need – To Be Preferred

"You shall not commit adultery." Exodus 20:14

This commandment guards a legitimate need to be ***preferred or significant to someone in particular***. If this need is violated, it brings the deepest wounds of distrust and **betrayal** plus a sense of being **uncovered** and **shamed**. It usually takes place because legitimate needs aren't being met within the marriage, and the person tries to get the needs met outside of marriage.

Frequently the physical aspects of this core need are preceded by the emotional and spiritual relationships. **Spiritual adultery** is lack of intimacy with God. It brings lack of trust in God and lack of faith.

We need to develop our intimacy with God through prayer, through worship, through trusting in His words to us, and through obedience. The farther we walk with Him in a journey of intimacy, the more we discover that He is faithful. We discover that He is faithful to solve our problems and to meet our needs. Our relationship grows until the intimacy is fulfilling.

Now in this area, as in most of the other areas, the spiritual and the natural can't be completely separated. The need to be preferred by someone in particular will not be completely fulfilled without preference coming through another human being.

Let's use the example of a woman who is not the preferred person in the life of her husband. Perhaps the first person in his life is his mother, or perhaps it is a friend. It could even be another woman. How can she deal righteously with the situation? How can she look through her husband to God as her source of preference.

Any human being through whom that preference comes is only a channel for God to use. A human being cannot be the source. The important thing here is where she ***anchors her hope.*** She can't anchor her hope in her husband. If she tries to anchor her hope and expectations in him, she will end up judging him and suffering great hurt and bitterness. She must look through her husband and anchor her hope in the faithfulness of God. She must release all her judgments against her husband and all her expectations concerning him. Here are some practical steps to anchoring her preference in God:

- Decide to trust God... to trust His faithfulness.
- Daily nurture this "decision to trust" in God by praying, reading in the Bible, etc.
- Daily nurture forgiveness towards your husband (review keys to forgiveness and confess the forgiveness daily).
- Get help from a skilled marriage counselor to continue working on the relational issues

8. Core Need – To feel Secure

"You shall not steal." Exodus 20:15

This commandment guards the **legitimate need to be provided for...or to feel secure.** Each person needs to be **provided** for. We need to know that someone is looking after our well-being. Every man with a job, who is the provider for his family, still needs to be provided for. Now we're not saying that everyone doesn't have a need for provision. The need is that the source behind the provision is a secure source and will not run out or fail. Even the "bread winner" of the family needs to know that he is being provided for by God. He needs to live free from the fear that his source will run out. He needs to know that his welfare doesn't depend on his ability to hold a job.

This legitimate need is met illegitimately when a person is **self-sufficient** or when he looks at the channel as being the source. Again, the difference between a good work ethic and a **self-sufficient** person is the **motivation** within.

Matthew 6:19-21 "Do not lay up for yourselves treasures upon earth...for where your treasure is, there will your heart be also."

Understand that this is not to say that people are not to work and earn provision. It is the understanding of the heart that is important. We can trust in our ability to provide, or we can trust in God as our provider. *If we trust in God, we will not look at our jobs as the source of our supply.* We **work** in obedience, and **trust** for our provision. We will look at them as only the channel through which God is meeting our physical needs. If that job dries up, we are secure in the fact that the Lord will use another channel. Our needs will be met. The **self-sufficient** man sets God out of the picture and **trusts** in his own ability to meet his needs. So deep beneath the provision lies the heart of **security or insecurity.**

A second ingredient to **Security** is that of **protection.** This speaks again of our need for physical security. When the area of physical security or protection is violated during the formative years, that person invariably feels a type of abandonment... thus, the lack of the protectors presence.

The third ingredient to **Security** is that of **emotional stability**. This is probably the most forgotten ingredient of **Security**. This type of **emotional stability** involves a real *"connection."* Here are some keys to *"connecting"*:

(1) Be vulnerable & transparent – when you allow others to see the real you, there is an endearment which is produced... others want to know you and feel comfortable being with you. This involves allowing others to see your weakness and to see you process through your problems.

(2) Enter their world – the young people have an expression, "Do you feel me?" This expression identifies the very heart of this ingredient. A couple of keys to *"entering their world"* are to maintain *eye contact, undivided attention* and learn the keys of *empathetic listening*. Learn how to put yourself into their situation... into their feelings. Sometimes role-playing if helpful at this point... each taking the others position. A good measuring rod for *emphatic listening* is one question: *"When a mistake is made, what is your first or primary response... to instruct or to affirm?"*

9. Core Need – Integrity & Credibility

"You shall not bear false witness against your neighbor." Exodus 20:16

This commandment protects the legitimate need to **have the right things said about us, the need for Integrity.** The word "witness" is a legal or judicial term meaning "reputation." So this need speaks of your witness, your credibility, your integrity. What is said about you is important to each of us, because "we are only as good as our word."

Webster defines *"integrity"* as (a) *an unimpaired condition* (b) *firm adherence to a code of values* (c) *quality or state of being undivided*. So *"integrity"* is a quality of character that is defined by a single-minded and single-heart, holding to a moral value system, and maintaining an unimpaired condition.

When the Core Need for *integrity* is violated there is the loss of valuing and regarding one another. This means that there is a failure to treat one another as important... honoring one another. This **need to be respected** is violated by:

- Not giving the appropriate authority given for the level of responsibility within a relationship.
- Responsibility to do a job is given... but the freedom to do it your way is not given.
- Listening is accompanied by interrupting.
- You have no input into plans that affect you.
- No apology is given when wronged.

When this core need is being met, you have a feeling of value. The other party listens to you and solicits your ideas. When you talk, they listen intently... without interrupting. When they are wrong, they apologize.

10. Core Need – To Feel Content

"You shall not covet...." Exodus 20:17

This commandment protects **the need to be fulfilled, satisfied and content**. It is interesting that this is the last need mentioned in the commandments. So frequently, *contentment* is directly related to *purpose*. Purpose **is not a singular event or destination... but rather an ongoing process**.

Since there is a difference between seeing a purpose and fulfilling a purpose... due to the fact that many see purpose as a ***revelation rather than a process***. So lets begin to make some notes about the ***process of purpose which leads to contentment***.

***Purpose** produces passion ...* this produces *joy* in the journey, which produces *contentment*. So note again the 4-step process by which you live your life in continual *contentment*: (1) **Purpose** (2) **Passion** (3) **Joy** (4) **Contentment**.

Now a beautiful note about the relationship of **Purpose & Passion** is that **Purpose** produces **passion... not the reverse!** A couple of young people get together and think that they are in love… so they have a night of passion and from that passion comes a baby. Later they realize they are not in love and don't want to get married. Their passion did not create purpose… only problems!

So we have to be careful in thinking that we come to a fantastic worship service and have a morning or evening of passion in the presence of God… and we walk away thinking that we are a people of purpose… yet the purpose never comes to definition or articulation…and that is because purpose always proceeds passion.

Wherever there is purpose, there should be passion. The passion goes out the marriage when the purpose goes out of the marriage. The passion goes out of relationships when the purpose goes out the relationship. The passion goes out of churches when the purpose goes out of the church. So purpose produces passion.

Purpose produces passion that produces joy in the journey! This means that you begin to love what you are doing. **Purpose** *produces* **passion,** *which produces* ***joy,*** *which produces* **contentment.** A significant ingredient to the recipe of Identity is the purpose unto contentment.

Now, the opposite of these four steps to the Process of Purpose

Task produces duty…, which produces resentment… which produces judgment! Here is the issue… when we lose the purpose, that which we once did because of purpose we now do because it is a task. So we do it because it is there to be done. Rather than because we want to do it…and the results is that we begin to live "dutyfully" to fulfill that task.

It happens all the time. People begin to come to church with a purpose. They have a love and passion for coming. They invite their friends to come and join in the fun. But there comes a time when they don't like something… and what was once a purpose, a passion, a joy… becomes a task & a duty. And of course what happens then is that produces resentment! I resent giving my time to being here when I should be…other joys are filling my life. Then the resentment leads to judgments where we begin to point the finger and gripe and complain and gossip.

The real problem is that somewhere amidst the journey, we lost the purpose. We keep on doing what we do… but our attitude has changed because our hearts have changed. Then when our heart is disconnected from purpose, we become discontent… and look for someone or something to blame. In fact, from that point on, we begin to criticize and complain about everything… because our heart is discontent.

What has happened? We have made the shift from **purpose** to **task**; from **passion** to **duty**; from **joy** to **resentment**; and from **contentment** into **judgment**. Now we begin to sneak around and we become a problem rather than a blessing… but we won't see that we are a problem… it will be someone else. We even become a problem to ourselves… because deep inside there is an irritation, which keeps us stirred, critical, and discontent… without purpose or contentment.

Understanding the Process of Judgment

Diagnostic Questions – What is your greatest judgment? When do you feel you have the right to express your opinion? *Are there weaknesses in your parents that you are finding manifesting in your own life?*
Prognosis – Judgments have a boomerang effect. You throw them out and they come back and hit you right on the nose… and you become the very thing you detest.
Remedy – Choose to trust God, rather than judge. Trust and Judging are opposites…with forgiveness in between them.

We have talked about the entrapments of iniquity, transgressions, and sin. Now we want to deal with the root of *judgments*. First, we need to understand what a judgment is. *Judgments* can range *from making a legal decision to simply forming an opinion*. Anytime we form an opinion, about ourselves or someone else, we are judging that person. When we speak that opinion, we are releasing the judgment. Maturity gives us a better basis for forming opinions, but even then we tend to judge by what we see and hear. We judge people by what we see them do, by what we hear them say, by those things that our five senses perceive.

When Sue does something, I judge her actions. When John does something, I judge his actions. But I judge myself based on my intent rather than my actions. In fact, if my intent is bad, but my actions turn out good, I'll reverse the criteria and judge myself by my actions instead of my intent. I give myself an amazing amount of latitude, but with others I judge strictly by what I see or hear. Do you see the inconsistency frequently found within the process of judging?

Even opinions formed on what the senses perceive do not produce dependable judgments. They do not allow for the intent of the heart. I Samuel 16:7 says that "...man looks on the outward appearance, but God looks at the heart." So there is a type of judgment based on what we perceive to be right or wrong, good or bad, based on criteria perceived through our five senses. It is based on the "tree of the knowledge of good and evil."(Genesis 2:17) The Bible says that type of judgment does not give life. But there is also another type of judgment.

John 7:24 says, "Do not judge according to appearance, but judge with *righteous judgment.*" "*Righteous judgment*" is that which agrees with what God sees. It is a judgment that is the result of *spiritual discernment* rather than *sensory perception.*

Jesus said in John 5:30, "I can do nothing on My own initiative. As I hear, I judge; and My judgment is just because I do not seek My own will, but the will of Him who sent Me." Again in John 8:26 it says, "I have many things to speak and to judge concerning you, but He who sent Me is true; and the things which I heard from Him, these I speak to the world." Even though Jesus was wiser than any other man who ever lived, He never issued His own opinion. He spoke only what His Heavenly Father said.

In the same is true with our own opinions. Our opinions do not give life. The only thing that brings life is the Spirit of God. So if we are not speaking something by the Spirit, then our words will at best be "right". In other words, we could have perceived the situation and released our opinion based on our knowledge and we could be right. That is the best we can hope for.

God-given *discernment* not only contains revelation of what God sees and says, but also the timing to speak. Being *right* does not mean that the other person is ready to hear what we have to say. His heart must be prepared. We do not release life by just *being right.*

We can perceive a situation and have all appearance of being right, but releasing our judgment won't bring life to that person because perception is not discernment or God-inspired timing. It is the presence of the Spirit of God that gives both discernment and timing. When we speak what God is saying, it may be a difficult word, but in the right timing, it will also give life.

Remember that God doesn't look at the outward appearance. He looks at the heart. He understands all the intentions and motivations behind the action. He is the only one with this discernment, so He then gives this *discernment* through the Holy Spirit. Even then, He does not always want us to speak the things He shows us. Sometimes He shows us things simply for the purpose of prayer. Other times He tells us to speak it forth to the person.

When this happens and *we say what He says* about a situation, we release *righteous judgment*. Remember such judgment cannot come from our sensual perceptions. It must come to us by what the Spirit of God speaks.

Righteous Judgment involves three things

(1) Holy Spirit *discernment* (2) Holy Spirit *timing*... These two ingredients both embodied in (3) the Holy Spirit's *anointing*.

The Greek word for *judgment* is "krino". From the beginning, this word never carried the idea of expressing one's own opinion. When Moses set up judges in the Old Testament, the judges were to judge by reading what the law said about the situation. The spoken word of God would judge the situation. They never released their own opinion in the judgment. Jesus never released His own opinion, but He released what He heard the Father saying. He released judgment by the Spirit, not by His own perception of right and wrong.

In Proverbs 28:5 it says, "evil men do not understand justice, but those who seek the Lord understand all things. " If our discernment is by the Spirit, our judgment will be with understanding, not based on appearance. Why? Because we are listening to the Spirit of God who is judging the heart. He sees a larger picture. Proper judgment, properly applied, provides right discipline and gives life.

Many parents have learned that they cannot discipline their children based on the children's actions. Sometimes their wrong actions have pure intent, and the parents shouldn't discipline those actions in the same way that they discipline a wrong intent. Sometimes their actions are not really bad, but their intent is very bad. Even in disciplining children, it is important to judge by the Spirit.

So as we read the Bible, we find some statements that appear to be very contradictory concerning judging. Some encourage us to judge while others say don't judge. They are not really contradictory. They are just talking about judging which is based on sensory perception as opposed to judging based on spiritual discernment. Let's look at a couple of them.

Understand Your Realm of Authority

Matthew 7:1-2 "Do not judge lest you be judged. For in the way you judge, you will be judged; and by your standard of measure, it will be measured to you."

1 Corinthians 5:12 "For what have I to do with outsiders? Do you not judge those who are within the church?"

<u>2 Critical Parts to Every Judgment</u>
- *Your Realm of Authority*
- *Your Criteria from which you judge*

Understand that there is a balance to "Do not judge." It has to do with how the judgment is made, and it also has to do with **the realm** in which you release your judgment. Paul was expecting the elders at Corinth to speak judgment *within their realm of responsibility*.

We need to understand that there is an *area of authority*, in which people are responsible to *discipline* or *release judgment*. It is a God given legitimate authority, such as a father has for his children or elders have for a church. It does not have anything to do with "judging" those for whom we have no responsibility and over whom we have no authority. Paul talks about it in 2 Corinthians 10:13 when he says, "...But we will not boast beyond our measure, but within the measure of the sphere which God apportioned to us as a measure, to reach even as far as you."

The Apostle Paul is talking about a measure or a *sphere of authority.* There is the responsibility to release judgment within our *sphere or measure* of authority. Our *measure* is our *sphere of responsibility.* If we want to understand where we have authority, we have to clarify our *responsibilities.* Who looks to us for provision and protection? If I am a father, I am responsible for my family. If you are single, you may only be responsible for yourself. Our *sphere of authority* is delegated in accordance with the *position of responsibility* that we fill. Within the church, God delegates responsibility to elders to judge within the local body. In families the husband is the delegated head of the family. The wife also has a *measure of rule* over the household. These are delegated *spheres of responsibility.*

Spheres of Responsibility

Each one of us even if we do not have children and even if we do not have a delegated position within a church, still has spheres of responsibility. Many people own businesses and are in charge of things in their businesses, or perhaps where they work. Everyone has at least one sphere of responsibility, which is himself. *Everyone is ultimately responsible for himself.* The apostle Paul said, "...But let each man examine himself, and so let him eat of the bread and drink of the cup. For he who eats and drinks, eats and drinks judgment to himself, if he does not judge the body rightly. ...For if we would *judge ourselves*, we would not be judged." 1 Corinthians 11:28-32

If we take the responsibility to judge our own behavior and our own motives, we will not need to be judged or disciplined by others. We always have the right to judge ourselves. We also have the right to release judgment within *our sphere of authority,* **our** *measure of rule.* But we do not have a right to release judgment *outside* our measure of rule. We have no right to judge the actions of our parents, our friends, our pastor, or anyone else for whom we have no responsibility. ***When we release our discernment outside of our sphere of responsibility, we have moved from discernment into judgment.***

When we try to release judgment outside of our responsibility, we are not ensured accurate discernment. If it isn't within our measure, God is not obligated to give us sound judgment. There are a lot of pieces of the picture that we simply can't see because it is not our responsibility. We may see some things very correctly, but because it is not our *sphere*, we may not have clarity of the "big picture".

Remember that we were talking about a parent judging his children through God-given *discernment*. Because God has given the parent authority over those children, He is also able to give him clarity of *discernment*. With this *discernment*, we will be able to see the intent of the situation and the attitude more than just the actions. So there is a time for "right judgment".

Using Discernment Outside Your Realm of Responsibility

There is a situation where it is okay to release judgment outside of your sphere of authority. If someone asks us for our help and opens the door for us to speak into their lives, we can do so, even if they are not within our measure of rule. They are the *doorkeepers* of their own life. They are giving us the "authority of honor". They respect us and want to hear our discernment.

If we feel that God wants us to speak something into the life of someone who is not within our responsibility, we must always issue it in form of an *"appeal"*. An *appeal* always comes in the form of a **question** or general statement that might be something like this, "John, this is what I believe that the Lord is showing me about your situation. You will have to discern for yourself whether or not it is something that you should receive." This type of statement does not come from a position of authority, but more like a **suggestion**.

Judgment & Boundaries

"What if the individual has been hurt by the parent and this assessment or evaluation is simply a defensive step prior to setting boundaries?" There is a step prior to setting a boundary. It is necessary to evaluate and determine the source and effect of behaviors that are destructive in order to properly set a boundary. But even then, the "discernment" and "information" used to make this determination is not released outside your realm of authority and responsibility. There are *two good "determiners" that will help you discern if you have made a judgment*:

(1) *Do you feel pain when you think about that person, circumstance or event?* If you do, chances are that you were wounded and most likely that wound has precipitated a judgment.

(2) Is your "discernment" or "information" which is used to make this determination attached to a negative or positive thought or feeling? If it is attached to a negative thought or feeling chances are that you have made a judgment. For example, do you treat your children the way you do because you have a conviction of a principle in scripture? Or, do you treat you children the way you do because you have a bad memory of a time your parents treated you the opposite? The former is attached to positive "information" while the other is attached to "negative" information which is most likely a judgment.

Judgment & Discipline

Hebrews 12:5-8 "...My son, do not regard lightly the discipline of the Lord...for those whom the Lord loves He disciplines...God deals with you as with sons... if you are without discipline, then you are illegitimate children and not sons."

God disciplines His children. Illegitimate children are those children who won't receive discipline. They run from discipline. They won't become accountable, so they jump from place to place always on the fringes. It is because they will not receive discipline. They have a ***spirit of illegitimacy***.

So a legitimate son will always receive discipline. As a matter-of-fact, a right son with a right heart will seek the Lord's discipline.

Understand the Purpose of Discipline

Hebrews 12:9-11 "...we had earthly fathers to discipline us, ...yet to those who have been trained by it, afterwards it yields the peaceful fruit of righteousness."

Discipline is a "**partial release of judgment**", not all of God's judgment, just the part that He wants us to deal with at the time. This judgment reveals an area that needs correction. The word *'to be trained'* means "*to practice naked*." It comes from a word that was used in the Greek referring to "**the athletes that trained in loincloths**." There is a transparency that is developed when we are trained by discipline. It takes away our masks and false identities. It takes the sin out of the hiding place and exposes it. Then the sin or weakness can be dealt with. This is the training of discipline. When we are trained by it, "afterwards it yields the peaceful fruit of righteousness." (Hebrews 12:11)

Discipline & Bitterness

It is interesting that the most famous of verses dealing with "bitterness" if found here amidst the topic of discipline. Hebrews 12:12-15 says, "that no root of bitterness springing up causes trouble, and by it many be defiled." Frequently bitterness is due to wrong discipline, or what was perceived to be wrong discipline.

The problem begins when parents, teachers, employers, pastors, and others release discipline within their responsibility, but out of their own bitterness, out of their rejection, or out of their frustration and anger. They cause deep hurts and wounds and even speak forth curses over the lives of others. For example, parents who call their children "stupid" or "lazy" until the child believes it and forms his life in agreement with the parent's opinion (judgment). This is the reason that it is important to learn to release only *discernment from the Holy Spirit.*

Why People do not Receive Discipline

1. To rightly receive discipline, the first thing we will need to resolve is the origin of the authority. Romans 13:1-3 says "Let every person be in subjection to governing authorities. For there is no authority except from God and those which exist are established by God ...For rulers are not a cause of fear for good behavior, but for evil." This passage says that **all authority is set in place by the Lord.**

Two things from this passage:

- All "authorities" are placed by God.
- Do not fear. When a person fears authority, it is usually for one of two reasons: (1) There is something within he does not want exposed (2) There is the lack of trust and faith in God.

2. To receive discipline the second thing we must understand is that **discipline is not dependent on the maturity or spirituality of the one in authority**, but rather is dependent on our response. Everything is dependent on my reaction, not on the godliness of that authority. We must learn to look through the vessel and see the hand of God. We need to ask ourselves, what is God trying to say or show us through this situation?

So how do you respond to discipline? When I know the discipline is right, I confess the sin and adopt steps of correction. But if I do not feel that the rebuff is right, I might respond by saying, "Thank you for sharing that with me. I will certainly pray about it." If I have been honest and my heart is open to correction and instruction, I will ask God what I need to do. I don't worry about it or dwell on it, but I try to stay open to His correction. In this way I am not looking at the authority, and I am not judging that person. I am looking to God. He is our final authority.

Judging the Spirit of the Situation

We must also judge the spirit of the situation, and address the presence and influence of the enemy. If I am a parent with a child who struggles with anger, and all I do is discipline the child when he is angry, the anger problem will not be broken. We must cut off the tie and the energy behind it. We must bind the spirit of anger and cut it off from the child. It must change in the spiritual realm in order to change in the natural. It is our responsibility to release that judgment in both areas, the spiritual and the natural.

To Judge or Not to Judge?

Every believer has the responsibility to bring judgment against the works of the enemy. Let's look at it a little closer in two verses that seem to contradict one another.

> John 3:17 "For God did not send the Son into the world to judge the world, but that the world should be saved through Him."
>
> John 9:39 "For judgment I came into this world, that those who do not see may see; and that those who see may become blind."

In one instance He said, "I did not come to judge the world," and in the other instance He said, "For judgment I came." Every time you see an apparent contradiction in the word of God, know there is a balance to that truth. The balance comes in John 5:27.

> John 5:27 "...and He gave Him authority to execute judgment, because He is the Son of Man."

Jesus did come to execute judgment. He did not come to condemn, but He came for judgment. He came to execute judgment against the works of the devil in order to save you and I from judgment.

To understand this we have to see that judgment has two sides to fulfill one purpose. The ultimate purpose of the judgment of Jesus is to bring salvation and restoration to people. This means pointing out those areas in the lives of people that cause destructive behavior and getting rid of them. His tool of judgment is discipline and correction to bring more "**freedom**" and more "**life**" to the believer. If we ever find "judgment" taking place where the intent is *not redemption and restoration*, it is quite certain that this discipline and judgment did not come from God. God's intent is always deliverance. So the focus of judgment toward the believer is to bring about deliverance and restoration. In fact, the primary word translated "salvation" or "saved" is the Greek word that means "to deliver."

The other side of that judgment will be against the devil, to remove his bondages from that believer's life. Remember the enemy has already been judged (John 16:11). He is within our *"measure of rule"* as a believer. Still we don't release our own judgment. We release what God says. We have the right and responsibility to speak out against the enemy that which God is saying and that which He says in His word. We don't judge people. We judge the *action* of the person, and we pronounce judgment against the *spirit* causing the problem. This plan is seen in Psalms 149:8-9 where it says, "...To execute on them the judgment written..."

Let me give you an example. Let's say that I am a parent. My ten-year-old son has just rebelled against my authority. I need to both discipline the child and judge the spirit of rebellion. It is important that the child clearly understand that I am separating him as a person, from the spirit and attitude that he has cooperated with.. You see the two as distinctly different. Johnny is accepted and loved, yet the spirit he has listened to and partnered with, is rejected and judged.

It could go something like this:

"Johnny, do you understand the devil is our enemy and we don't want him doing his work around our house. He is not your friend. He is trying to make you be some one that you were not created to be. God made you to be obedient to your parents. What you did was disobedient. You don't have to give into the mean desires and ideas that the devil

brings. So I want to pray with you and we will ask God for forgiveness and tell the devil he is not our friend and he has to leave us.

Dear Jesus, thank you for loving us and giving us our family. Devil, Jesus, Johnny and I say you have to leave our family and our home alone. We are kicking you out now and you are not welcome. Our family is staying together with Jesus, but you have to go.

Johnny, you don't ever have to feel badly for this. Today Jesus forgives you and puts His arms around you to protect you and hold you. So the next time the devil gives you a bad idea or desire, you can tell him to leave you... that Jesus holds you in His lap, and the devil has to leave you. Do you understand? Do you have any questions?

If the child does not accept the suggestion to pray, or continue to run and disobey after your initial confrontation, it might be necessary to discipline him. After you administer discipline, take time to hug and pray with the child, reinforcing his *acceptance* and my *approval* of him as a person.

Remember God told the children of Israel that He would not give them "the land" all at once, but that He would deliver it to them "little by little", as they were able to possess it.

We, too, must possess the land of our hearts "little by little". He will not overload us or give us more than we can bear. We are responsible to take care of the area He is pointing out. We don't have to be *perfect* to be completely righteous before God, but God does ask for our obedience. This is why 1John says, "walk in the light as He is in the light, and the blood of Jesus will cleanse you from all sin."

Judgments & Your Standards

Another important understanding concerning judgments is that a judgment is based upon "*standards*". *Standards* are attached to our *value system*. According to our priorities we develop standards. Standards are like the "inches" on a yardstick. They are the increment by which we measure, according to our value system. Others use a metric system (another value system) and therefore have different standards.

But if we judge in the wrong way, according to any other standards and value systems, other than what God is saying, we're going to have the wrong standards held over us. This is the essence of Matthew 7, when it says, "we would be judged with the same standards we use".

Romans 2:1-3 "Therefore you are without excuse, every man that passes judgment, for in that you judge another, you condemn yourself; for you who judge practice the same things. And we know that the judgment of God rightly falls upon those who practice such things. And do you suppose this, O Man, when you pass judgment upon those who practice such things and do the same yourself, that you will escape the judgment of God?"

What these verses are saying is that there is a *principle* in judgment that when we place law over someone, for some reason, we will start doing the exact same things that we are judging in the other person. How many times have you heard of a preacher who preaches hard against a moral vice, only later to discover that he himself is practicing the very thing he was so adamantly against?

What we often find in ministering to people is that the things they hated most in their parents are being manifested in their own lives. People, who were beaten as children, beat their own children. A man, who hated his father's alcoholism, finds he can't control his own drinking. So along with *"trans-generational iniquities"* which were passed down to them, they have judged their parents and other authorities over them.

In order to stop this, the *"sowing and reaping principle"* has to be broken. What is the sowing and reaping principle? It is the *principle of the seed* that says that **a seed will bear fruit after its kind**. In other words if we sow beans, it will produce beans ... if we sow love, it will produce love. We also need to know that the seed will bear fruit in proportion to the amount of seed that is sown. All seeds need is to be watered, cultivated, fertilized to produce fruit. If we make a one-time judgment and stop there, perhaps that seed won't bear much fruit, but if we continue to judge, what we are doing is cultivating the field, watering the seed, and adding more.

If we want to stop that crop from developing, we have to come in and plow up that old crop. God wants to do that in our hearts. He wants to plow up the wrong judgments and prepare the soil for a new and better kind of crop. So we need to weed that stuff out. We need to pull those judgments up by the roots.

Practical Ministry

1. Write down on a piece of paper anyone whom you have judged outside your "measure of rule". Ask the Holy Spirit to bring to your memory any wrong judgments that you have made. Allow plenty of time for the Holy Spirit to bring the memories and work conviction.

2. Individually pray the following steps over each person and situation that you judged.

   a. Confess all bitterness and unforgiveness as sin. Receive forgiveness.
   b. Confess the judgment as sin. Receive forgiveness.
   c. Confess as sin taking the place of God as the judge. Receive forgiveness.
   d. Forgive and release people you have judged. This means to release them from your expectations. Re-establish your hope is in the Lord, not in them.
   e. Address the enemy and take back any ground given to him because of the above sins.
   f. Break the sowing and reaping principle. Declare that *because of repentance (change of how your think about the issue), you will not reap what you have sown.* Ask for God's mercy and grace.
   g. Pray concerning any restitution that the Lord would have you make in the situation, such as asking the person's forgiveness for having judged them.
   h. Pray blessings upon the person you judged.

Prayer to Break Judgments

"Father, I ask You to forgive me for judging my dad. He was not my responsibility. I was out of bounds. My judgment is sin. Lord, I confess the bitterness that has been in my heart as sin. I renounce it and ask that you not only forgive that bitterness, but also to cleanse me of it. I also ask you to forgive me for taking Your place as judge. I do not have that position or the rights of that position. Lord, I receive my forgiveness in accordance with 1 John 1:9 and receive your cleansing from all unrighteousness."

"Satan, I take back all the ground that I gave you by judging my father and all the ground that I gave you by bitterness and unforgiveness. You no longer have a place to work in me due to that judgment. I declare that I am free of all the results of wrong judgment."

"Lord, please bless my father. Please free him from all results of my judgment against him and bring blessings into his life according to your grace and your will. In Jesus Name, Amen"

There is a final thought on judgments that needs to be added. It puts things in a little different perspective that will be helpful. God knew you, loved you, and chose you before the foundations of the world (Ephesians 1:4). He had a plan for your life even then. His plans and purposes for every life are perfect. They form a unique and specialized inheritance, which God has for each individual.

This inheritance fits the personality, gifts, and abilities that He has placed within the person. He knows exactly what path in life that person must take if he is to find maximum fulfillment and maximum joy. If God's plans were worked out perfectly, each person would experience perfect fulfillment, but sin entered the world, so people do not fulfill God's plans and purposes perfectly. Nevertheless, it is against these perfect plans and purposes that God determined even before that person was conceived that each person would be judged.

People fulfill these plans and purposes in varying degrees. Since only God knows the plan that He set before that life, only He can judge to what degree the person fulfills the plan. He may reveal a part of His plan to someone who has authority over that person and ask that person to speak this plan into that area of the person's life. Rightly receiving from that authority will help the person find the right path to God's good inheritance and destiny for him.

God entrusts us into the hands of various authorities. He knew us before the beginning of the world. He had already chosen us, so in a very real sense, we belonged to God before we belonged to our parents. He entrusted us into their hands for a time. He had a righteous standard (value system) by which He wanted them to raise us, but only He has the right to grade them on how well they met His standard. We do not have that right. Better still, it is not our responsibility. When we connect to Jesus, we put ourselves in a position to receive the inheritance that God had for us. Our inheritance is from Him, not from our natural parents.

As we come to know Him, to trust Him, to learn to hear His voice, and be guided by His Spirit, He can lead us into the fullness of our inheritance and destiny. Our hope is in Him. Our purpose is from Him, and our ability to fulfill our purpose is by Him. It is not our responsibility or concern to judge any authority whom the Lord gives place in our life. It is our responsibility to seek Him and to allow Him to speak to us and to discipline us directly or through those authorities if He so chooses. Whether or not they fulfill their part righteously or not, we can fulfill our part righteously, by looking through them to see the Hand of God. God has a special inheritance for each one of us. I want all of my inheritance...I want to achieve my destiny... how about you?

Understanding an "Offence"

Diagnostic Questions – Do you have any unresolved offences? What was the cause of the offence?
Prognosis – Offended relationships are often seen in other relationships. In the areas that you are offended once, you are susceptible to repeated offence.
Remedy – Forgive! Keep focused on the Big Picture! Trust God! Choose to not get offended.

Do you believe that God has a Destiny for you? When God told Israel of her destiny, he then told her to "follow the cloud." The cloud of His presence was to lead them into their destiny. But did you notice where the presence of God led them? God led them straight into the wilderness.

A spiritual wilderness is a place of no presence of God. It is a place of no revelation. A place of "heat"…difficult relationships and circumstances. It is a place of snakes and scorpions. A place of unrelenting attack by the enemy…everything you try doesn't seem to work. It is a place of constant fatigue and stress… everything seems hard.

Jesus went to the wilderness but only for forty days. Whether or not you go to the wilderness or not is not an option; but how long you stay there is. Forty years, or forty days, the decision is yours.

So why does God take us into the wilderness? In Deut.8: 2 it says, "And you shall remember all the way which the Lord you God has led you in the wilderness these forty years, that He might humble you, testing you, to know what was in your heart..."

The issue is the **heart**... the wilderness is the place of surgery on the heart. He says God sends you into the wilderness to: **Humble you** - humility is a conscience awareness of your inability, with a simultaneous awareness of His ability.

"See what is in your heart" - God knows what is in your heart... He wants you to know what is in your heart. What is in your Heart? I trust many good things... but Ex.34: 7 speaks of three things, not so good, which God forgives:

- **"Iniquity"** which literally means "the bent, propensity or *desire* of sin"
- **"Transgression"** which occurs when the "will consents to the *desire*"
- **"Sin"** which literally means the "action or activity of a *desire*"

Most of our Christian lives focus on the *sin* issues... *sins* of omission and *sins* of commission. Sin is like the fruit on a tree. We are constantly trying to take off the bad fruit and put on the good fruit. If sin is the fruit, then *iniquity* is the root.

The difficulty is that because *iniquity is a desire*, you cannot see an iniquity, so it is difficult to know where iniquities hide in your heart... so you can deal with them before they become fully manifested sin? There are three passages I want you to look at:

Ezekiel 14: 3 "Son of man these men have set up their idols in their hearts, and have put right before their faces the stumbling block of their iniquity." Note carefully, the words "stumbling block" or literally, *"rock or stone of stumbling"*. What is this *rock of stumbling*?

Then again in Ezekiel 18:30 (last half of the verse) "...Repent and turn away from all your transgressions, so that iniquity may not become a stumbling block to you." So there is something called *a rock or stone of stumbling* that is connected to iniquities. What is the *stone of stumbling*?

Take this thought through the cross and into the New Covenant. 1 Peter 2: 6-8 "Behold I lay in Zion a choice stone, a precious cornerstone, and he who believes in Him shall not be disappointed. (7) This precious value, then, is for you who believe. But for those who disbelieve, the stone which the builders rejected, this became the very cornerstone, (8) and, a stone of *stumbling*, and a *rock of offence*;"

What is a cornerstone? It is a stone placed in foundation by which the sides are brought into alignment. It is also, the top last placed stone in an old Roman archway.

It says, "He who believes..." There are areas of our lives that we don't believe in? In these areas the cornerstone becomes something else... the rock of stumbling? If you read carefully you will note another name for the process of stumbling... offence. Have you ever been *offended*? Why did you get offended? We get offended because we think we are right and they are wrong!

Have you ever noticed how consumed we are with the idea of being right? Where did we get this insatiable desire to be right? Back in the Garden of Eden, there were two trees. One was commended by God and the other was prohibited by God. These trees were called, the *Tree of Life*, and the *Tree of Knowledge of Good and Evil* (literally, "that which is morally right and morally wrong"). So in the areas of our hearts where we are preserving our "right-ness", in these areas, we are offend-able.

Also note, the only places in our hearts where we can be offended are areas where iniquity resides. Let me say it differently... ***every time you get offended, it is because of iniquity hiding in that area of your heart.***

For those of you that have relationships to the Catholic Church, I need to make one extra note. The Catholic Church teaches a concept that you can offend God, and that is why you have to do penitence. Never in Scripture is the word *offence* used in relationship to God... because God does not have iniquity.

One more verse, Luke 17:1, Jesus is speaking to His disciples and He says, "It is inevitable that stumbling blocks (offences) should come..." In other words, ***if you can be offended, you will be offended!***

Some Examples from the Bible of people getting offended:

- Genesis 4:1-8– Able was accepted and Cain was not, therefore he got offended.
- 1 Chronicles 13 - David was bringing the Ark into Jerusalem. When the Ark passed over threshing floor it shook and those walking alongside it reached out to steady it. At a result of touching the Ark, two men died. David did not understand why God would allow these deaths, so David gets offended over an issue of Divine order.
- John 6: 52-61 – Some did not understand the teachings of Jesus, and were offended because of this.
- Matthew 11: 1-6 - John the Baptist was in prison at the end of his life. He was about to be be-headed for serving God. God did not come through according to his expectations and as a result he was offended.

Even with this understanding on offences, the reality is that many of us have in fact been wounded by offences. Lets make one special note...*offences do not wound; but wrong responses to offences wound*.

There are two noted parts to every offence. The first part is an **unfulfilled expectation**. When expectations go unfulfilled, there is always the opportunity to get offended. The only way to keep away from the disappointment of unfulfilled expectations is to look to Jesus to meet your needs.

A second part of an offence is a **violated right**. A *right is the result of imposing my standard (values) on my perceived need."* Where do standards come from? Some standards are taught. Other standards come from judgments (see chapter nine). In addition, a last source of standards is from what the Holy Spirit is speaking. 2 Peter 1:12 says that God will "establish us in the truth that is present"... or, "present truth". So it is what the Holy Spirit is speaking to us at the moment that keeps us stable.

What if we have been offended? How do we get un-offended? The key to unraveling an offence is *forgiveness*.

Note Six Keys to Forgiveness

- Forgiveness is a choice, not a feeling.
- We don't forgive because they are worth it – we forgive because He asked us to forgive.
- We do not forgive out of our own resources, but from the mercy He has given us.
- We must release expectations / rights (Mt.18:27).
- Hebrews 10:18 says, "where there is forgiveness, there no longer remains any offering for sin." The word "offering" literally means "a price to be paid; something to be done." So when you say to someone, "I forgive you" you are releasing him or her from any further responsibility of response.
- Where necessary, forgive yourself.

What you speak is what you get!

Diagnostic Questions – What nicknames have you been called? What derogatory statements were made about you as you were growing up?

Prognosis – Words contrary to the purpose and plan of God for us have the potential power to hold us locked in their cycle…especially if they were spoken by authorities in our lives.

Remedy – The power of a curse is in the authority of the one speaking the words… therefore the remedy is to break the words spoken and speak blessing in place of the curse.

To understand curses and how to deal with them, we need to understand that there is a *realm of blessing* and there is *a realm of the curse*.

Deuteronomy 30:14-20 "…I have commanded you today to love the Lord your God, to walk in His ways, and to keep His commandments, His statutes, and His judgments, that you may live and multiply, and the Lord your God will bless you… I have set before you life and death, blessing and cursing; therefore choose life…"

The Lord made it clear that there is a realm of blessing and a realm of curse. The children of Israel stayed in the realm of blessing by simply doing what God asked of them. The Lord had already commanded, through Moses, an effective demonstration of these two realms as they applied to the old covenant. (Deuteronomy 27) Joshua carried out the demonstration, when they arrived in the

Promised Land, by dividing the people into two groups. (Joshua 8:30-35) One group stood on Mount Ebal where the law of Moses was written on stones. The other group stood on Mount Gerizim. The ark of the Lord was in the middle. Joshua, apparently along with the Levites, read all the blessings and the curses. When a curse was read the people on Mount Ebal would say, "Amen". When a blessing was read, the people on Mount Gerizim would say, "Amen". They were saying, "So be it."

These people were rehearsing their commitment to the Lord. They were agreeing that if they kept the Mosaic Law they would be blessed, and that if they did not, they would be cursed. They understood how to stay in the realm of blessing and how to leave it for the realm of the curse. As you read these "curses" we can see what Jesus has delivered us from.

Instead of being under this old type of law, we are under a new law...the law of the Spirit. The law for us is that which the Lord has *written on our hearts*. We are to walk in obedience to what the Spirit of God has spoken to us personally. He can bring that revelation to us by speaking through the scriptures, or by using other people to reveal what He is saying or simply by impressing a thought or feeling upon our hearts. We are not responsible for things that we do not know until the Lord brings conviction (convincing) that a thing is wrong, but we are responsible to obey the things that we do know.

We stay in the realm of blessing by cooperating with all we have been shown. We break our relationship with Jesus and step into the realm of the curse by transgression, by knowingly ignoring what God asks of us. Even if we sin, we can get back into the realm of blessing by simply confessing the sin (1 John 1:9). Only by refusing to change when we are convicted of sin do we keep ourselves in the realm of the curse.

With this basic understanding of the general realm of the curse, let's address the issue of spoken curses. Most of the time we encounter curses, we will be dealing with word curses. So let's deal just a little with the power of the spoken word.

The power of the spoken word is very dependent upon the *authority* of the speaker. If the speaker has no *authority*, his words carry no *power*. What God speaks forth always comes-to-pass because He has all authority, and He is the one who delegates authority. All authority is delegated by God.

The gospel of Matthew tells a story about a centurion who came to Jesus. He had a servant who was sick. He asked Jesus to heal his servant, and Jesus said that He would go and heal him. The centurion said, "No, you don't have to come with me. I too am a man under authority. I tell this servant to go here and he goes, and I tell another to go there and he goes. You simply speak the word, and my servant will be healed (Mt.8)." Jesus then made a statement that he had not seen such great faith in all Israel. What was he talking about? The man understood that the word of Jesus would carry power based on His authority.

Jacob was a very interesting guy. He wanted his brother's birthright. He also wanted his brother's blessing. However, it is important to remember, the blessing was spoken by the father near his point of death. When Isaac found out that he had spoken the blessing over the wrong son, it was not recanted. Jacob went to a lot of trouble to receive something that was not tangible. It was just some spoken words. But Jacob understood that there was a realm of authority that his father carried, authority assigned to him by God. The authority was such that if he would speak the blessing, it would come-to-pass. He recognized the power and the authority of his father's words.

So when a person has been given authority in a situation, their words carry power based on the sphere of that authority.

In the book of 1 Samuel, it says that Samuel carried a great deal of authority from God. The Bible says the Lord didn't let any of Samuel's words fall to the ground (1 Samuel 3:19). That meant the Lord used His authority to fulfill all that Samuel spoke. His words carried authority.

In Numbers 22 through 24, we find the story of Balaam when Israel came to the Valley of Moab. Moab hired Balaam to curse Israel. They made a statement like this to Balaam: "Balaam, whomever you curse is cursed and whomever you bless is blessed." Balaam corrects the statement later when he begins to prophecy. He said, "How can I curse whom God has blessed?" In other words, if God has not cursed it, it cannot be cursed. The boundaries of both curse and blessings are set by the spoken authority of God. We cannot place anyone in either realm by the word of our mouth, unless they are under our authority. So your authority determines the extent and degree of the power of your words.

Another important truth about the realm of the curse is that the curse is the domain of Satan. Satan has authority in the realm of the curse. He has no authority in the realm of blessing. Balaam came to curse Israel, and as long as Israel was dwelling in that realm of blessing, he could not curse them. No matter what he said, all that came out was blessing. God had commanded Balaam not to speak anything that God wasn't saying. If God didn't say it, Balaam wasn't to say it.

Balaam was a seer-type prophet. He could see the future. He knew what was going to take place. Having the knowledge did not give him the right to speak it forth. Just because God has shown us something, we don't have the right to speak it unless God sanctions it and gives us that authority. But Balaam took the authority that God had given him as a prophet, and he misused it to speak something that God did not give him permission to say. What he did was to speak of the power and might that Israel would have in the future, which was the truth, but God didn't tell him to say it. Why? Because it told Moab more than God wanted them to know. As a result the Moabites totally changed their tactics.

They decided that they could not overcome Israel by war, so they came in and intermingled with the children of Israel. They intermarried, and because of that, the Israelites began to worship some of those Moabite idols. In doing so, Israel took themselves out of the realm of blessing and placed themselves in the realm of the cursed. Twenty-four thousand people died from the plague that resulted from that curse. Even then the plague would not have been stopped had not Phinehas taken a stand for God and reproved the sin.

The negative words of people's mouths will not carry authority with us as long as we are in the realm of blessing, but as soon as we step into the realm of the curse, if those people have authority in our life, their words will have power. Word curses that have effect have frequently been spoken by mothers and fathers, or other authority figures.

In the same way, if our pastor says something to us, it carries more weight than some stranger that we meet on the street. If he comes up and tells us that we are stupid, we are much more likely to receive it than if the same words were spoken by some person we never saw before. Why? We just discount what someone says that we don't know or respect. But if it is someone that we respect and hold as an authority in our life, we are very likely to receive those words. Once we receive them, they will carry weight. So the power of the spoken word is dependent on the level of authority of the speaker.

If God has given the person the authority to speak the words, they are very powerful. But it also possible for us *to give a person authority which God has not granted*. This can happen in two ways. The person may be a legitimate authority in your life, for instance a parent, who is delegated as an authority for us by the Lord. But it is possible for that person, like Balaam, to speak words over us that God did not speak. Sometimes amidst the frustration of parenting, parents call their children stupid, or a liar, or lazy. The parent himself is a legitimate authority, but the words he is speaking are not in agreement with God's word and are not authorized by God for that parent to speak. This person has authority but the words do not. The child does not have to receive such words although he must retain respect for the parent. Such words are a curse, and if the child is walking in the realm of blessing, he does not have to receive such a curse.

The other possibility is that *we can give a person a position of authority in our life to whom God has not given such authority*. An example of this is peer pressure. Let's say there are some teenage girls who are friends. One girl knows that what the others want to do is not right. She doesn't want to do it. But when she indicates that she doesn't want to, they begin to tell her that she is stupid, that she is prudish, that she will never have any fun or any friends if she doesn't participate. So she goes along with them. What has she done? She has given authority to people who have no God-given right to influence her. She has put herself in the realm of the curse because she received what someone without authority said over her.

We need to understand that God's word, whether spoken to us through the Spirit or through His written word, takes a higher place of authority in our life than any human being. We should obey God first. Then, there are authorities that God has delegated for our lives, such as parents, elders in our local church, husbands, etc. They have a place of legitimate God-given authority, and we need to obey them, unless what they are telling us contradicts the higher authority of God's word. There are other people who would like to control and manipulate our life, including friends, boyfriends or girlfriends, people in the church, etc. If we choose to submit ourselves to them we can. God does not agree with it, but He will allow us to do it. By our choice, we give them authority in our life. Then their words will carry a lot of weight. When such people speak negatively about us and we receive what they say, we give them the power to curse us.

So what do we do with a curse? When someone has had a *word curse* spoken over him, and he has received those words, allowing them to take affect in his life, we must go back and break the power of the words. We must declare that these words have no affect. Since we are dealing in the spiritual realm we are not hampered by time. Time is a "sense world" commodity. You can go back and deal with a thing that happened in the past without any difficulty. When we go back to break word curses, we go back to the time those words were spoken, and we declare that they are powerless. We command them to *fall to the ground* and break their effect in that person's life.

Steps for Breaking Verbal Curses

1. Have a vital real connection with Jesus - Where you have been responsible, confess sin and receive forgiveness.

2. Verbally break the curse with something like this:

"Because Jesus is my friend, I am choosing to stand with Him and I am choosing to believe what He has said about me and what He has done for me. I am no longer cooperating with your lies in my life. "Fear" you will no longer run my life, I demand that you leave. "Fear" I break your power in my life. I am now standing with Jesus… a place of blessing.

3. Renounce all the ground the enemy has gained through that curse.

"Devil, you no longer have legal right to my life. I am standing with Jesus, and He holds me. Because I am standing with Jesus, you have no power over me or my life."

4. Replace the sin with a blessing.

"Dear God, thank you today for Your forgiveness and Your blessing in my life." (Replace the negative with the positive. For example, replace bitterness with forgiveness, etc.) It is frequently helpful to think on different Bible passages about your specific area of weakness. We call this "taking a *God-look*." Allow what you read and discover to bring strength and healing.

Vows & Inner Determinations

Diagnostic Questions – What destructive cycles of behavior are you unable to stop? What "internal determinations" have you made?
Prognosis – Frequently offences and wounds precipitate internal determinations…i.e. "I will not marry someone like my father/mother;" " I will not treat my children the way my parents treated me." Take a pencil and paper and list the "internal determinations" that you can remember from your earlier years.
Remedy – After discovering the vow, break the judgment and replace the vow with a commitment of blessing.

Vows are very closely related to judgments. Frequently where you find a vow, there will also be a judgment. The difference is that judgments are usually turned outward. They judge other people. A vow is turned inward. It is a determination of the heart concerning oneself. A vow is actually saying, "I don't want anyone, not even God, to control this part of my life. I am going to take control of this part myself so that I myself can protect and guard this area of my life." Vows are made because of what someone else has done to us, and that is why they are connected with judgments.

For example, a young girl is mistreated sexually. She not only places her judgment on the person who abused her, but she also vows in her heart that no man is ever going to touch her in a sexual manner again. What has she done? She has made a determination of the heart. Her purpose was to protect herself from any further hurt and degradation, but in actuality she has taken the authority for one area of her life and removed it from God's authority and, therefore, from His covering. Perhaps she does not tell anyone else of her determination, and perhaps she forgets she ever made it. Nevertheless, the thing is programmed into her life. She has set the course of her soul and given direction to her mind, will, and emotions in that area of her life. Later she marries, and discovers that she cannot give herself to her husband, as she desires to do. She just can't release her affections to him, especially physically. Programmed within her soul is a determination not to allow any man to touch her sexually.

She may not even remember thinking that, but it is there, rising up and hindering what she wants to do. She is now a Christian, and she prays for God's help in the situation, but it seems that the Lord won't help her. She has made a vow. She has set her will against the physical affections of men. She has taken the right to rule that part of her life out of God's control, and He will not touch it until she breaks the vow and gives Him the right to control that area of her life.

Many times in counseling if we come up against an area that simply will not break, look for a vow. Ask God to reveal any vows that may have been made to affect that area of the person's life.

Psalm 95:8 says, "Do not harden your hearts." Inner vows are part of a hardened or stony heart. An inner vow is the most unyielding part of the habits built into our flesh. It is a determination and directive into our inner being, which controls and blocks our soul from being able to follow after the will of God. They hold us, causing the way we feel, think, and act to be as that vow previously determined.

Vows Are Connected To Judgments

Vows are connected to judgments. "*I will not be like my mother. I will never drink like my father did. I will never marry a man like my father. I will never let a woman hurt me again. I will never be embarrassed like that again.*" Not only does the *judgment* need to be nullified as we talked about in the section on *judgments*, but also the vow must be nullified to give God the right to restore that area of our lives to His control and well being.

Even though, as an adult, we may understand why our parents or others acted as they did or treated us as they did, it doesn't affect the vow. We may have even forgiven the person and received healing from the incident, but the vow remains intact because it has never been nullified. Our attitude may have changed completely as an adult, but we must remember that the vow may have been made based on the perceptions of a child. Vows are made in agreement with what we perceive the situation to be at the time. Whether or not the perception was accurate, the vow has power to hold on to the soul until it is broken. It puts a hard, untouchable place in the heart. But, thank God, He knows how to deal with stony hearts. "I will give you a new heart and a new spirit within you; I will take the heart of stone out of your flesh..." Ezekiel 36:26,27

Steps To Breaking A Vow

1. **Recognition** - Ask the Holy Spirit to reveal to you any vows that you made. Ask Him to bring to your memory any such situations or any such determinations that you may have made in your heart.

2. **Repent** – Repent for any sinful reactions which caused you to make the vow - hate, resentment, vengeance, judgment, bitterness, fear, shame, etc. *Repentance* means to change how you look at it... change your perception.

3. **Confess it as sin** – This is where you "own" it. Confession literally means that you agree with God about what you did or said or thought.

4. **Nullify the vow verbally** – There is something about hearing yourself speaking out the opposite of the vow. This expression might sound something like this: "Because I am now standing with Jesus, this resolve from my past no longer has power over my life."

5. **Recommit your life to Christ**. It is simply transferring trust for your life to Jesus.

6. **Replace with God's Word**, which puts God's control in the area where the vow was in your heart. Stand firm in what the word says and in keeping your heart fixed on God.

Boundaries

Diagnostic Questions – What areas of your life do your feel others violate your right to make decisions and express opinions? How well is "no" accepted in your relationships?

Prognosis – Frequently when boundaries are violated the individual does not have the freedom to develop and express his/her own personality… their own uniqueness.

Remedy – Boundaries must be set to give room for health and growth in different areas of life.

Understanding "boundaries" brings completion & balance to the teaching on "**offences**" (chapter eleven). We ended offences with talking about forgiveness: (1) A Choice (2) Not because they deserve it (3) Out of His mercy given to you… not your own resource (4) Heb.10: 18 "Where there is forgiveness of these things, there no longer remains any offering (literally, *a price paid; something to be done*) for sin." (5) To complete forgiveness, you must release your being right (6) forgive yourself where appropriate.

This type of definition, though accurate, leaves us feeling vulnerable to hurt again. Therefore it is important not only to forgive… but the individual is also responsible for his/her own spirit and conscience, because bitterness has a devastating consequence.

So the balance to complete forgiveness is not some measured or qualified forgiveness, i.e. "I'll forgive you but….", rather, the balance is found in the use of boundaries.

In this time of "following the Spirit" there seems to be an incredible loss of boundaries. Under the auspices of "Liberty in the Spirit" there seems to be a blatant disregard for individuals boundaries. People unreservedly give advice where they have no responsibility. People are rude and ungracious under the disguise of Honesty. People give "personal prophecies" without permission of the person... and even many times, without permission from God.

Do you know what judgment is? Remember Mt.7: 1 says, "Judge not lest you be judged for in the manner that you judge it will be met out unto you." Judgment is simply "releasing your discernment outside your boundary of responsibility."

Webster defines "boundary" as "something which indicates or fixes a *limit* or *extent*; a *separating line; that which keeps some things in an other things out.*"

- **Fixes a Limit or Extent** – to enable *function and proper growth and development*
- **A Separating Line** – Keeps some things in and other things out – *protection*

So in these days of change, days of "new wineskins" and "new wine," God has given incredible, timeless "Life" giving tools that we are not to abdicate... and one of these "Life" giving tools is a thing called "*boundaries.*"

So many destructive encounters in life are in fact a result of a violation of a boundary. For example, an emotional breakdown is usually the result of a failure to place or enforce boundaries within ones emotional life.

In Galatians 2:7 Paul speaks of his destiny and of Peters destiny... and he says, "But on the contrary, seeing that I had been entrusted with the gospel to the uncircumcised, just as Peter had been to the circumcised." Because of boundaries around his destiny, Paul knew what was *not* his destiny... as well as what was his destiny! Do you know what is *not your destiny*? If you do not, you will spend great amount of time working on good things... outside the boundaries of your destiny.

Pr.8: 29 says, "When He set for the sea it's boundaries so that the water should not transgress His command." So just as there are *physical boundaries* ... there are also boundaries in every "sphere or arena" of life.

So, first lets note three types of Boundaries, then we will see four arenas of life these boundaries exist in.

Three types of boundaries

God Placed Boundaries – Ps.74: 17 says "Thou hast established all the boundaries of the earth."– All natural boundaries are in fact God placed boundaries. For example, the Ten Commandments are in fact, God placed boundaries.

Man Placed Boundaries – Saying *"NO!"* is the setting of a boundary for another. Covenants entered into are mutually agreed to boundaries. Man placed boundaries are only binding to the extent the other is within the boundaries of that specific authority.

Demonically Placed boundaries – Do you know what Spiritual Warfare is? It is the removal of boundaries set in place by the enemy... and the enforcing of boundaries set by God, challenged by the enemy. Remember, Pr.26: 2 says, "without a cause a curse cannot light." With cause, the enemy can place and enforce boundaries in our lives.

Four Spheres of Life

ARENA ONE is the **INDIVIDUAL**. 1 Corinthians 6:19 says, "Or do you not know that your body is a temple [temple, house, sphere, arena] of the Holy Spirit who is in you, whom you have from God, and that you are not your own? For you have been bought with a price: therefore glorify God in your body." The first arena is the individual, and each individual is composed of three parts... body, soul and spirit, each having boundaries.

If you violate a boundary of the body, you get wounded or sick. If you violate a boundary of the soul (mind, will, emotions) you become sick of "heart." When you violate a boundary of the spirit, you become spiritually ill.

ARENA TWO is the **FAMILY UNIT**. A key to finding these "areas" or "spheres" is that each one has a *"head"* that is giving for the protection of the boundaries. Eph. 5:23 says "For the husband is the head of the wife, as Christ also is the head of the church, He Himself being the Savior of the body." Within the family unit, there are boundaries not only for their protection but also to enable their function and proper growth and development.

There are many scriptures that speak of the function and proper growth and development of each family member… these are given not as suggestions… but rather as functional boundaries to enable proper growth and development. "Children, obey your parents"… "Children, honor your father and mother"… "Husbands love your wives"… "Wives, submit yourselves to your husbands"…"fathers, do not provoke your children to anger"… family, "submit yourselves one to another"… etc.

ARENA THREE is the local **CONGREGATION**. In 1 Corinthians 3:16 " Do you not know that you ["you" plural… all of you] are a temple of God, and that the Spirit of God dwells in you? " So within the local congregation there are boundaries. For example, most of 1 Corinthians 12, and 1Corinthians14 [and many others] are simply boundaries set forth for the proper function and growth of the local congregation.

In 1Peter 5:3 there is a boundary set for Elders in the use of authority… and it speaks of being an example, not lording … "nor yet as lording it over those allotted to your charge, but proving to be examples to the flock." So there is a very clear boundary for an elder as to how he is to use his authority.

Another boundary within this **ARENA THREE,** the local **CONGREGATION**, is found in 1Timothy 5: 19, and it says, "Do not receive an accusation against one in the assembly, i.e. a complainant at law; spec. Satan: - accuser] especially against an elder except on the basis of two or three witnesses." Here a very clear boundary is identified concerning what we are to say about an elder in a local congregation... even if we think they are doing something wrong.

ARENA FOUR is that of the **KINGDOM OF GOD**. In John 14:2 Jesus says, "In My Father's house are many dwelling places; if it were not so, I would have told you; for I go to prepare a place for you." This fourth arena is that of the Kingdom of God Universal.

A much overlooked Kingdom Boundary is found in Mt.18:18 "Truly I say to you, whatever you [plural] shall bind on earth shall be bound in heaven; and whatever you [plural] loose on earth shall be loosed in heaven." This fantastic truth of binding and loosing is keyed not for the individual as many use it, but rather for the corporate body. There are some functions that are reserved for the corporate body and not given to the individual due to the need of balance provided by the corporate.

So there are four arenas in which we experience boundaries. Now remember, the failure to understand and use boundaries can result in destructive behavior. Boundaries are key to restoration. Boundaries are also essential to discipline.

Now, before we identify the four key dimensions in which boundaries are found, we need to understand one primary difference in definition.

Freedom or Liberty

Freedom and Liberty: you can have freedom without having liberty. Freedom is achieved by removing some boundaries, and putting other boundaries into place. Freedom requires the act or action which removes the boundaries which enslave us. Liberty requires the act or action that removes the boundaries that limit us.

Freedom is the result of experiencing the TRUTH ("you shall know the truth, and the truth shall make you free"), while Liberty is the result of experiencing the SPIRIT ("where the Spirit of the Lord is, there is liberty").

While freedom removes shackles which cause us to act destructively; liberty removes shackles which keep us from the fullness of God's provision

So with these understandings, let's note the four dimensions in which boundaries are found.

Four Dimensions in which Boundaries are found

The first three dimensions are well known and agreed upon by all scientists:

1. The first dimension measures HORIZONAL distance – think of a horizon...
2. The second dimension measure VERTICAL distance – think of the clouds in the sky... the distance off of the face of the earth.
3. The third dimension became well known in the fifties ... "3-D Movies came out" – the dimension of *depth*. These 3 dimensions together determine "volume."
4. But it is this Fourth Dimension that brings us to a current and present day search.

The fourth dimension is that of *time and space* – at least this is how the scientific world identifies it.

"Time and space" is also know as a *"simultaneous dimension."* This dimension does not recognize the normal boundaries, as we know them. Remember the scripture says, that to the Lord "a day is as a thousand years and a thousand years as a day." It became obvious that when Jesus walks through a door and suddenly stands in the room of disciples in Luke 24, that space no longer has a boundary that contains Him. Therefore, somehow, this fourth dimension is an overlay or *simultaneous dimension* upon all the others.

It is also important to remember that after the resurrection that Jesus would allow Thomas to touch Him to prove he was not a ghost [a fourth dimension being]; He ate fish on the seashore to again prove he was existing in all *four dimensions*.

So think on this fourth dimension for just another moment. How was water turned to wine? Something happened that cause the water to no longer be subject to the boundaries of the first three dimensions... and move into the *fourth dimension.*

How was Phillip translated? He stepped over the boundaries of the first three dimensions and moved into the *fourth dimension*!

How did Peter and John heal the blind man at the temple? They moved into the *fourth dimension.*

Keys to using Boundaries

1. **The word releases and sets boundaries.** When God created the world He *spoke* the boundaries into existence. Some boundaries are eternal. God *speaks* and *His word* places a boundary. For us, "No!" is frequently a word of boundary.

In Romans 10:9-10 it says, "that if you confess with your mouth Jesus as Lord, and believe in your heart that God raised Him from the dead, you shall be saved; for with the heart man believes, resulting in righteousness, and with the mouth he confesses, resulting in salvation." The word "confession" comes from two Greek words ("homo" and "lego") which literally mean "to speak the same thing."
With the mouth speaking a word a boundary is set... a doorway is opened... into the *fourth dimension.*

Also, note about that *word*... it is a special type of *word* ... (10:8) but what does it say? " The word is near you, in your mouth and in your heart"— that is, the *word of faith* which we are preaching,". So not just a word, but a "word of faith."

2. **You can only place boundaries in an arena where you have God given authority.** Therefore, it is imperative to note different levels of authority, so you may know where and when to place a boundary (see pg. 75, "Seven Levels of Authority")

Understanding Your Level of Authority

Seven Levels of Authority

In the book of Daniel 3:1-6, we find a king commanding that people worship his image. Not to do so is to violate the law of the land. What would you do? In verses 16-18 Shadrach, Meshach, and Abednego say they will not worship the king's gods or his golden image. Are they in rebellion?

In the book of Acts, chapters 4 and 5, we find a description of Peter and John in trouble with the religious authorities because they refused to quit witnessing about Jesus. Are they in rebellion?

In Joshua 9, we find Rahab went against her government's edict to not let spies in. Was she in rebellion?

In 1 Samuel 16 we see Samuel was loyal to Saul, a rejected king who would not obey God. God had to pry him out of disobedience.

In 1 Samuel 19:1 God commands children to obey their parents. What should Jonathan do?

These passages bring up clear questions about authority issues. We must learn the truth about authority and walk in freedom.

Now let's turn our attention to a most important passage of scripture: Romans 13:1 *"Let every person be in subjection to the governing (superior in grade or level of authority) authorities."*

Now for study sake, I want to divide authority into two type of authority: directive authority [used primarily, but not exclusively, with the devil]; and secondly, indirect authority [used primarily in our relationships with each other].

Five Levels of Direct Authority

1. *The authority of God's presence-* Frequently when Moses was contested, God would tell the people to go to the tent of meeting... then God would manifest His presence so as to silence the contention. There is an authority resident in Gods manifest presence.

Now, the enemy also has a counterfeit of each authority. For the authority of God's Presence, the enemy's counterfeit is "peer-pressure" - have you ever noticed people who act differently when certain ones are around, especially ones that have authority? This is an authority of presence. So the lesson that we learn is, when the manifest presence of God shows up, everyone quits arguing... we must learn to defer to the anointing on another.

For example, in a worship service, even though the pastor may be preaching, when the anointing come upon another and they began to prophesy, for that moment, the one prophesying is in the position of "higher authority." In a marriage, although the husband is designated by scriptures as the "head" of the family, when the anointing is on the wife, she is in the position of "higher authority" for that moment or event.

2. Authority of God's Word (Truth — God's word) John 17:17 says, *"Sanctify them in the truth: Thy word is truth."* In Acts 17:11 The Bereans were taught by Paul and Silas and, *"They received the Word with great eagerness, examining the Scriptures daily, to see whether these things were so."*

Again, the enemy has a counterfeit, which are his lies, which lead to deception. His lies are not always obvious and overt; they are usually hidden partial truths, or twisted truths. At this level of authority, the enemy has another counterfeit...the *traditions* of man (Mk. 7:6-13). The lesson that we are to learn is that God has a present, current, relevant Word for each of us, and that *present word* carries authority. Remember 2Pet.1: 12 says that we "have been established in the *truth which is present* with us."

3. Authority of Conscience - The authority of conscience is not perfect or complete authority. One's conscience does not always reflect the perfect will of God. Romans 2:14-15 says, *"For the Gentiles who do not have the law do instinctively the things of the law, these not having the law, are a law to themselves, in that they show the work of the law written in their hearts, their conscience bearing witness, and their thoughts alternately accusing or else defending them."*

That is why Paul could then say in Romans 14:23 *"But he who doubts is condemned if he eats, because his eating is not from faith; and whatever is not from faith is sin."* 1 Corinthians 8 passage speaks of not eating meat sacrificed to idols, and of declining meat if it offends your brother because . . . v. 12-13 *"and thus by sinning against the brethren and wounding their conscience when it is weak, you sin against Christ. Therefore, if food causes my brother to stumble, I will never eat meat again, that I might not cause my brother to stumble."*

So Paul speaks of how eating this sacrificial meat was causing some young Christians to stumble, thus he exhorts the more mature to honor the authority of the weaker conscience. Now the enemy also has a counterfeit, which are feelings and pleasures. From this we get the expression, "If it feels good, do it!" This is an expression not of a godly conscience, but rather, the enemy's alternative.

One more note about this level of authority. We defer to another conscience within the parameters of our own conscience... as well as the higher authority of the Word. This level of authority is key to developing relationship of intimacy. When we are attempting to walk with another, and their conscience is violated by something we do, no matter how right we may be, we need to learn to defer to their conscience, within the parameters of our own conscience.

4. *Delegated Authority* - This is the first place where human authority comes into play. Matthew 28:18 says that all authority belongs to Jesus. Any authority that man has is at best delegated authority from Jesus. The key word to delegated authority is "responsibility"... these are two sides of a single coin. Thus, when you look for an elder, find a man who is already serving the people... as an elder... one who has received the weight of responsibility to serve without any title... then recognize what God has already made him and give him authority. This is the level of all governmental authority. As with each authority, the enemy also has a counterfeit for this level...it is *usurped authority*. The lesson we are to learn from this level of authority is that we are to honor the delegate, as we would honor the one who sent him.

5. *Authority of Legal contract or covenant* - If you ever doubt this level of authority just try to not make a payment on a car or house that you signed a contract to pay... see if the contract has a level of authority. One day you might wake up only to find that your car is no longer sitting where you left it!

The enemy has a counterfeit for this level of authority, and it is legalism. Never before has legalism been such the problem as it is today. God is seeking to move His body into covenant relationships, all the while the religious crowd continues to set up standards... leading to legalism. The lesson that we must learn is that we are to defer to another contract... in fact the scriptures say that we should simply operate by a word... a "yes" or a "no". We must learn to keep our word and give enough grace and liberty to allow others to keep their words.

Now we want to move to two additional authorities... **Indirect Authorities**

6. *Functional Authority* - This is authority that comes by ability... ability that comes by gifting, talents, education, or special knowledge. Example: Home - Watch the great apostle at home when the baby cries-Who is in authority? Not the great apostle, but the mom. Example: Church — Watch the elder who knows nothing about the demonic bow to the guest speaker when a demon manifests.

Example: If we were to have a car-wreck out here on the road, and people were injured... soon three people arrive, a policeman, a doctor, and a mechanic. Now, who has authority to direct the traffic? Who has the authority to help the injured people? Who has the authority to see if the car can be towed?

It is also interesting to note that this is a servant's authority. In Bible times, each servant was taught a skill or trade, and that skill was his realm of authority. But remember, Romans 13: 1, *"Let each be in subjection to the higher in grade or level of authority..."* So that means that gift authority is always subject to governmental authority.

Now the enemy does have a counterfeit to this level of authority, and it is *Lording*. *Lording* means there is no mutual submission. So we must learn to defer to gift, to function, to ability..."submit yourselves one to another in the fear of Christ."

7. Authority of Honor - Honor means to esteem valuable and precious; to respect. Here the one under authority opens the door to the other person's authority because of honor. In relationships of maturity the authority of honor is the guide by which all walk. If you are married, what level of authority do your parents now have with you as a married couple? Ephesians 6:2 says, *"Honor your father and mother (which is the first commandment with a promise).* They now have authority to the degree that you choose to honor them.

The same is true with apostolic ministry and a church... only to the degree that the elders and pastor receive and honor that gift, does that man have authority in that church. The difficulty with honor occurs when the one that is to be honored, is not honorable. When one has been abused by an authority figure, such as a parent or grandparent, it becomes very difficult to honor that parent or grandparent, until the issues of offence and abuse have been addressed, healed and restored.

Now the enemy does have a counterfeit... dishonor. Literally that lack of giving honor is usually the epitome of self-honor. So the lesson and guideline for us is to learn to honor. This is an important and valuable lesson.

Boundaries can be destructive as well as constructive

Sometimes when we say "no" it can result in healing. But when the "no" is left too long, it can become a place of hiding from reality. In the United States, we have a legal term known as "The Statue of Limitations". Simply stated, there is a time limit by which you can be prosecuted for a crime. In the spiritual and emotional realms, it says basically the same... there comes a time when you must say "enough is enough." Draw a line and do not return that way. So the boundary can give a place of health and growth... but like a cast on a broken arm, if left too long, can atrophy the muscles.

In addition to speaking the word, there are sometimes actions of obedience to release or enforce the boundary. For example, when God spoke to Joshua that all the places his feet would tread would be his... He still had to go walk. Joshua walked seven times around Jericho because Jericho was the biggest and most fortified city in Canaan, he wanted to be very sure it was his. So he put *action* to his faith and words.

Setting a Boundary

So how do you place a boundary or remove a boundary? To be simply stated, boundaries are placed by the spoken word. But sometimes there are actions or higher levels of authority that are needed to enforce or support these "word" boundaries.

1. Speak the word. When a boundary is needed, speak the word of boundary to anyone "bordering" that boundary. For example, if you are married, and you feel like something asked by your spouse violates your conscience, then speak the word "no."

- If boundaries are not a normal part of your relationship, an explanation and discussion might be required. If necessary, solicit a "third party" involvement to guide the conversation into an objective and constructive direction.
- Discussion and mutual agreement can place boundaries in an amenable way.

2. Act the word. Boundaries are not only placed verbally, but sometimes they are placed by your actions. One of the best examples is that of *making decisions…*or *not making decisions.* Frequently in a relationship, the activity of making a decision can establish a boundary… or the abdicating of this decision-making process can leave the door open for boundary violation. This type of relationship is frequently referred to as a "Jezebel-Ahab" relationship. The reference denotes a king, who would not take up his responsibilities as a king, thus leaving the door open for the illegal operations of his wife, Jezebel.

3. Appeal to higher authority. When the boundary is not honored, it may become necessary to appeal to a higher authority to become involved to enforce the word. Every level of authority has a responsibility to enforce the boundaries of that level.

- Frequently in counseling situations I invite the client to acquire a third-party accountability to aid him/her in the enforcing of their personal boundaries.
- In a marriage situation, the input of godly parents is frequently helpful in maintaining the integrity of the family boundaries.
- In extreme boundary violation where a life is in danger, civil authorities can be called in to enforce the boundaries that protect life.

4. Removing a boundary that is for specific protection should only be considered when the neighboring parties have demonstrated sufficient health and restraint to walk without such a tool.

- When a specific protective boundary is being removed, it may be helpful to have another person serve as a guardian for a period-of-time. This "guardianship" would consist of a type of daily accountability. Depending on the severity of the previous violations, this would entail either a telephone call or a personal visit.
- When removing a boundary that you have placed on your own life, a counselor's oversight is helpful for the rehabilitation process. For example, if you have been abused in a dating relationship and put a "no dating" boundary for a period of time; when the boundary is removed and you are attempting to re-engage the dating scene, a counselor's aid is most helpful during this process.

5. Don't forget the boundary of God's Word. One of the greatest benefits of reading the Bible is gaining insight to the many different boundaries that God has placed for our health, growth and protection. These boundaries comprise the border of what the Bible calls, the realm of "blessing."

Ouch! It Hurts!

Diagnostic Questions – Has someone offended you that you have had trouble forgiving?

Prognosis – Wounds are not always visible. The beginning of treatment begins with the discovery and admission of the existing wound.

Remedy – Because one of the major defense mechanism for dealing with wounds is to suppress or forget the wound; we must begin by asking God to uncover and disclose the wounds… even ounds that occurred in the womb.

Different pains are determined by different types of wounds. A cut, a hit in the nose, a skinned knee, a broken arm, a gun shot… all the wounds are different, exerting different types and levels of pain. A wound is literally "that which violates the integrity of the organ."

Isaiah 53:5 says "But He was *wounded* for our transgressions, He was *crushed* for our iniquities; the chastening for our well being fell upon Him, and by His *scourging* we are healed."

Some special notes on this verse:

"Wounded" literally means "pierced through" or "punctured"

"Crushed" literally means "to collapse or break"

"Scourging" was usually accomplished with a "cat of 5 or 9 tails" – a small whip held with one hand, the leather had bits of bone or metal interlaced, so the desired effect would be as the whip hit, the bones & metal would rip the skin leaving open lacerations.

A wound is "an injury, especially on in which the skin or other external organic surface is torn, pierced, cut or otherwise broken." Frequently the difficulties of life cause us to get wounded. These wounds are a result of different causes... with different effects. Even though they are not necessarily physical, the emotional wounds are just as traumatic and often times leave lasting scars.

A Few Different Types of Wounds

Abrasion – "a wearing away by friction." Frequently life will afford us some precious relationships, which are better defined by "iron sharpening iron." These are the types of relationship that if given a choice you will avoid. You may or may not like them... but that there is always disagreement and tension. This type of tension causes a constant rubbing, a friction, and an abrasion. This is not life threatening, but very uncomfortable.

Piercing / Puncture – "to puncture, pierce or make a hole." In the passage from Isaiah 53, the word translated "wounded" literally means to pierce or puncture. The difference between a piercing and a puncture wound is that a piercing wound goes in one side and out the other, leaving a free flow to the blood. A puncture wound goes in one side but not out the other, therefore, the bleeding tends to be internal. A piercing wound has the danger of the loss of too much blood, but the benefit of being a "self-cleaning" wound. A puncture wound on the other hand will tend to have the danger of infection due to the inability to clean itself.

An emotional piercing wound is one that goes completely through you leaving you feeling somewhat empty. A death can be somewhat a piercing wound. Your heart bleeds for a season then slowly the pain subsides...but there is always the scar, the memories of that person.

An emotional puncture wound is one where the offence is held in. The pain can be deep, but there is no release or forgiveness... the results is usually the infection of bitterness. This type of wound is most dangerous because it has not only the ability to infect the one injured, but also has the ability to defile others.

The puncture wound, if infected with bitterness, frequently has to be opened up and drained. This "opening up" can either be voluntarily or sometimes is the result of further pressure or injury. If this wound is not opened, it will not heal. Opening is achieved by releasing the right or wrong-ness... and forgiving.

Laceration – "to rip, cut or tear." This type of emotional wound occurs when another speaks wrongly of you. It is usually not life threatening, but leaves a scar. If the cut is large enough, it will require stitches... a process that keeps the wound immobile for a period of time. Emotionally, when you are cut, you might have to have a season of solitude from that relationship in order for the proper rest to take place for healing. When a "soul-tie" is dissolved, frequently this type of wound occurs on one side (breaking off an affair, divorce, etc.).

Break/Fracture – "to crack without separating into pieces... but to render unusable or inoperative." When there is an emotional "break" there is needed a season of immobilization.... followed by a type of relational therapy prior to reconnection. Sometimes within a marriage this type of wound is experienced. Verbal and emotional abuse cause a "break" emotionally, and trust is lost. When this occurs, there is usually a time of "separation" needed (immobilization). After some time of rest, new relational skills need to be acquired. Then when the emotions have strengthened, and new skills acquired, a reconnection is possible.

Bruise – to injure without breaking or rupturing. An emotional bruise is sometimes slower to heal than a laceration. Bruises occur when there is excessive pressure, which causes internal hemorrhaging and hypersensitivity in that area. An emotional bruise is sometimes slower to heal than a laceration. Sometimes the bruising occurs within the process of discipline... when God is attempting to correct an area of character, and the process is incomplete, frequently our resistance to His direction creates bruises in our hearts and lives. Other bruises are the results of offences and judgments. A bruise is healed with time and the removal of pressure.

Wounds and the Womb - Some wounds occur in the womb. Crisis and duress that occurs while pregnant, has the ability to "bruise" the emotions of the unborn baby. Ministry for this type of wound has to be usually through a word of knowledge. Adoptees have a higher rate of "inter-uttero bruising" than others do. Because one of the major defense mechanisms for dealing with wounds is to suppress or forget the wound, we must begin by asking God to uncover and disclose the wounds...even wounds that occurred in the womb.

Some of the most difficult wounds to overcome are the wounds that have been inflicted while in the womb. From thousands of hours in the counseling room to hundreds of research journal papers by psychologist and psychiatrists, the facts are confirmed that some destructive behavior patterns can be associated and connected to traumatic experiences while in the womb.

Of all the types of destructive behavior patterns, violent or self-destructive behavior seems to be the type most easily documented to stress and trauma experienced while in the womb. Due to the lack of information as to the exact relational & emotional climate during the pregnancy, there is a great deal of difficulty in documenting scientifically, the pressures and traumas experienced in the womb.

Beyond the documentation by professionals, I have found that the wounds, especially bruises, received during the time in the womb, are real and serious and not to be taken lightly. When I suspect that the present behavior is related to an experience in the womb, I approach the client in a different way.

Because we are "spirit-natural" beings, we have the ability to work in both the natural realm as well as the spiritual realm. In the natural realm, we are limited by time and space. In the spiritual realm we are limited by neither time nor space. Because of this lack of limitation, we are able to effect healing across the expanse of time and space.

This process is frequently part of what has been called "inner healing." The ministry consists of praying and speaking (prophesying) to the "child" within. Remember that time does not exist in the spirit realm, so there is not a problem speaking across time to the child within the womb. If we are aware of the exact nature of the problems at the time the child was in the womb, we speak directly to the spirit and soul of the little one within the womb, affirming and reinforcing the character and presence of Christ in the womb.

For example, when we discover that abandonment occurred while the child was in the womb (the father left), our prayer might be something like this:

"Father, I thank you for this little one. I thank you for the destiny that holds this child. In the name of Jesus, I speak to the baby in the womb and declare to you that you are fearfully and wonderfully made. You have been created for destiny and you are valuable and wanted. You are much desired. Daddy God loves you and draws you close to his heart. Daddy declares to you I love you and will never leave you for forsake you."

After praying this type of prophetic prayer, I then proceed by asking the client to picture in their mind Daddy God... however they conceive Him to be... sitting on a throne, or with His arms outstretched in welcome... see Him in the spirit of your mind. Now see yourself climbing into his lap and being help by Him. Feel His breath upon you, and hear His heart beating. He loves you and greatly desires you. This visualization is an important step.

These small steps are critical in aiding the client in processing the wounds that have occurred in the womb. When those bruises have produced ongoing destructive behavior, it may be necessary to pray and speak to the "heart of the child" through the formative years of life as well as the time in the womb. I frequently find that as I am praying, God will give exact ages, timing, and the exact conflicts to pray for.

One afternoon I received a call from a young lady that had been molested as a child. Before she came in for her appointment, I was asking God about her condition and the Lord impressed me to ask her about her natural father (she was adopted by her stepfather). When she arrived, we began the appointment with a simple "debriefing" concerning the present problem. She was experiencing continual problems in her male dating relationships. When she paused in her story, I asked her to tell me about her natural father. She stared at the floor for what seemed to be and hour, then finally responded, I don't know my dad, he abandoned us before I was born.

Further conversation revealed that not only was she abandoned by her real father, but also during the remainder of the pregnancy her mother was involved with two other men, both abusive in the language and demeanor. As a result, after she was born, she desired the affection of men, but was afraid of men. The fear caused her to be manipulative while seductive. Relationship after relationship found her in abusive physical relationships... all the while feeling incomplete and abandoned.

As we began to pray, I felt impressed to pray for a little girl in the womb... then a four year old... then a nine year old... then a fourteen year old... then a sixteen year old... then an eighteen year old. After I finished praying, she looked up at me with tear-stained cheeks and asked, how did you know the exact times that our family had problems. Each of the times represented either a move or another significant time of stress.

The specific praying and speaking to the unborn child and the young child during its formative years was critical in the healing process for this young lady. The other issues of her heart and life were critically connected to the bruises of these early years.

More concerning the process of "inner healing" will be discussed and demonstrated in the level three seminars.

The Process of Healing

There are four critical steps to the process of healing:

1. "CONFESS" literally means *"to say the same thing" as*... as God says... about your sin. 1 John 1:9 says, "If we confess our sins, he is faithful and righteous to forgive us our sins and to cleanse us from all unrighteousness."

"Say the same thing as God" in three areas:

- It is sin – call it what God calls it

- I repent – to change the mind… not "penitence" or an act of contrition to gain grace and forgiveness
- I'm forgiven

It takes only one party in an offence or violation to accomplish this stage.

This step results in the offender being relieved of guilt and condemnation. Frequently if the offender has not received forgiveness from Jesus, confession seems to easy… remember though, that even confession does not acquire the forgiveness, it simply opens your heart to receive the forgiveness.

Confession should include only those offended… confession is as wide as the circle of offense.

Remember that different types of wounds require different types of healing. The two great needs of wounds are cleaning and immobility. Infection and lack of closure are critical, therefore this step of confession both to God and to man is indispensable.

2. "RECONCILIATION" means "to make both different."

2 Corinthians 5:18-20 says, "Now all these things are from God, who reconciled us to Himself through Christ, and gave us the ministry of reconciliation, (19) namely that God was in Christ reconciling the world to Himself, not counting their trespasses against them, and He has committed to us the word of reconciliation. (20) Therefore, we are ambassadors for Christ, as though God were entreating through us; we beg you on behalf of Christ, be reconciled to God."

It takes both parties to accomplish this step. This step results in the BOND OF PEACE between the two parties. Remember Paul said to do your best to live at peace with all men. Reconciliation is not always possible. But your part in the process is possible… and you must trust God with the other party. (Romans 12:18, "If possible, so far as it depends on you, be at peace with all men.")

Frequently the greatest obstacle to this step is the knowledge that you are right. To be reconciled, you must have a greater desire to reconcile than to be right.

3. "RESTITUTION" literally means "to repay, to give back so as to complete."

Exodus 22:1-5 says, "If a man steals an ox or a sheep, and slaughters it or sells it, he shall pay five oxen for the ox and four sheep for the sheep. (2) If the thief is caught while breaking in, and is struck so that he dies, there will be no blood guiltiness on his account. (3) [But] if the sun has risen on him, there will be blood guiltiness on his account. *He shall surely make restitution*; if he owns nothing, then he shall be sold for his theft. (4) If what he stole is actually found alive in his possession, whether an ox or a donkey or a sheep, he shall pay double. (5) If a man lets a field or vineyard be grazed [bare] and lets his animal loose so that it grazes in another man's field, he shall *make restitution* from the best of his own field and the best of his own vineyard."

Proverbs 6:30 says, "Men do not despise a thief if he steals to satisfy himself when he is hungry; (31) but when he is found, *he must repay sevenfold*; He must give all the substance of his house."

Numbers 5:6-8 says, "Speak to the sons of Israel, 'When a man or woman commits any of the sins of mankind, acting unfaithfully against the Lord, and that person is guilty, (7) then he shall **confess** his sins which he has committed, and he shall make **restitution** in full for his wrong, and **add to it one-fifth of it,** and give it to him whom he has wronged. (8) But if the man has no relative to whom *restitution* may be made for the wrong, the *restitution* which is made for the wrong must go to the Lord for the priest, besides the ram of atonement, by which atonement is made for him."

Restitution or *repayment*, means *"to be in a 'completed' state."* The thief *replaces* what was stolen seven times.

This stage of healing takes only one party. Note that if the person is not available; give it to the Lord. This step is critical to the *return of the value* of the relationship (trust). Frequently the occasion occurs where one violates another in a fashion that is not tangible; therefore restitution is not so easily seen. For example if you were unfaithful in a relationship, how do you make restitution?

Remember that *restitution is for the offended*, therefore, ask God to show you what type of gift or sacrifice would have *meaning to the offended.* I had a man in one of my churches, who was in that position. He had been unfaithful to his wife. When he asked the lord what to offer for restitution, the Lord told him to sell his golf clubs and commit that time weekly to his wife. The wife saw that something of value had been given.

This step is critical in the restoration of a broken trust relationship.

4. RESTORATION means to return, but in greater fullness, quantity and quality.

God's *restoration is always greater in quantity and quality.* Job 42:10 says, "The Lord *restored* all Job had two fold."

At this stage the *function and fitting* are completely restored. Frequently when a relationship is broken the relationship is first *reconciled...* but then a season of time occurs for full *restoration* to take place. Remember frequently your failures cause wounds in others therefore, restoration may take time...time for others to deal with their own hears issues. So, *continue to sow until restoration is complete.*

Practical Help to Healing Life's Hurts
- May take time
- Seek to Understand, but do not base choices on this understanding
- "Journaling" is helpful
- Support groups are helpful in the processing
- Don't make decisions apart from counsel
- Rehearse God's faithfulness

Defilement, Soul Ties, & Heart Writing

Diagnostic Questions – What smells, old songs, etc. bring back "Deja Vu" for you? What feelings cause you to remember certain situations or relationships?

Prognosis – Frequently one of our senses tie us to a previous experience or relationship. When these are positive, they reinforce good memories. When these are negative, they hinder productive behavior within their sphere of memory.

Remedy – The ties to parts of our soul have to be "untied" and then reconnected or positively reinforced.

The greatest of life's difficulties does not come from the seen, but from the unseen; the covert, not the overt; the hidden, not the obvious.

On of the most amazing stories in the Bible is the account in Numbers 16 of Korah and his infamous rebellion against Moses. Most remember the account from the miraculous ending of the earth opening up and fire coming out and swallowing up Korah and his some 250 followers. What is intriguing is that Korah could get 250 leaders to follow him. How did he do that? These men were not children; they were leaders of the nation. They were men of influence and respect, probably representing some 250,000 people. Again, how could Korah get these 250 leaders to follow him in a coo against Moses?

In Hebrews 12:15 we find the well known passage concerning bitterness. "See to it that no one comes short of the grace of God; that no root of bitterness springing up causes trouble, and by it many be defiled."

It is interesting that this famous passage is found in the middle of a chapter about "discipline." Possibly, the greatest issues of bitterness are found within the crucible of discipline.

People given to bitterness frequently find themselves unable to keep their mouths shut. The result is what the Bible calls "defilement." In this case, "defilement" was the taking up of another's offence.

Mt.15 says, "that which comes out of the mouth defiles...". That which comes out of the mouth "defiles" both you and others. So gossip, slander, grumbling, whining...all these verbal communications have and incredible ability to defile.

Therefore, for defilement to take place all you need is a wounded or offended party; another party who will listen and the verbal communications from the wounded party. Therefore, defilement takes place in three ways:

1. By **conscious association** – Proverbs 13: 20 says, "He who walks with wise men will be wise. But the companion of fools will suffer harm."
2. By **unconscious association** – remember in Joshua 7 the "sin of Achan"? This one sin caused the entire people of Israel to loose a battle and many to die. They were defiled not by conscious association, but by unconscious association. Because they were in covenant with Achan, his defilement was spread to them.
3. The difficulty is that even the best intentioned are frequently defiled through what is called **"empathetic defilement."** With a desire to do good and be compassionate, we listen, only to find ourselves being persuaded and taking up the offence of the one we listen to. One of the most difficult lessons that a young believer will learn is how to put a guard on his/her ears.

Now with this in mind, let's look at another passage of scripture. 1Peter 1:13 says, "Gird the loins of your mind for action, keep sober in spirit, and fix your hope completely on the grace which is to come..."

Lets make some notes on this passage:

"Gird" denotes a belt / girdle used to draw together clothes in preparation for action

- "Loins of your mind" speaks of more than simple intellect, but *the imagination of our heart* where actions are born. Imagination is the womb where most actions begin. Loins are the seat of passion and pro-generative power.
- Ephesians 6 gives us the added insight that we are to gird out loins with "truth". This "truth" is more than what is right or correct, but literally is a reference to "reality." Therefore, the idea is that we are to **gird our loins, the imagination of our minds, with "reality."**

Soul Ties

For every area of our sense, i.e. hearing, seeing, smelling, etc. there is a "reality" that God wants to consume our minds. If we do not, a *"soul-tie"* results. This term "soul-tie" is a term, which gained popularity and recognition through the special covenant that David had with Jonathan. It says of these men that their "souls were tied" one to the other.

"Soul-ties" are not necessarily a bad thing. Many of us when we enter into marriage desire to find our "soul-mate"... the one whom our soul is forever knitted to... the one with whom we share the deepest secrets of our hearts. Only the most special of relationships is given to this state.

So, what is a "soul-tie"? It is a natural sense that triggers an old behavior pattern or feeling, thought or decision pattern. Is there a special song that triggers a special feeling within you? Is there a special perfume that triggers a special feeling within you? These are forms of soul ties.

I remember one time playing fast pitch softball. One of the guys offered me some tobacco. Wanting to be "one of the guys", I accepted the tobacco. On the next pitch, a ground ball was hit to me. I was playing third base, and the ball bounced and hit me on jaw. As a result, I swallowed the tobacco and promptly threw up. From that point forward in my life, I never seemed to be tempted by tobacco. Every time I would even smell tobacco, I would have a sensation to throw up.

So each area of our soul has the potential to be tied to something... and triggered by one of our senses: feel, sight, hearing, taste, and smell.

- **FEELINGS** – Frequently traumatized feelings, when touched by a circumstance or situation, revisit the old wound. The anger comes again, disappointment, loneliness, discouragement, rejection, lack of affirmation, abandonment, etc.

A man is raised by a dominating mother. Later in life, his wife begins to press him in their relationship, only to be met by severe outbursts of anger.

A daughter never held by her father tries to find comfort and approval in the arms of other men; only to find her life destroyed by the use and abuse of uncaring men. Time after time, she tries to find that which her father never gave her. The lack of approval, the lack of affection, never fulfilled.

I knew of a young staff member of a large church. His area of ministry was to homosexuals, himself being a former homosexual. One January he did not get a salary increase. Feeling that this was a sign of disapproval of his ministry, he began to feel the disapproval that once drove him into the homosexual lifestyle. Another staff member encouraged him to approach the Pastor for clarification. The Pastor was quick to apologize and correct the situation. This staff member learned a difficult lesson. A former wound, not completely healed, can tie your soul to that style of wound. Every time you entertain a similar situation, you feel the same old wound; the same disapproval; the same despair, etc.

- **SEEING** – TV, movies, magazines, all have the ability to tie your soul. This is the power of pornography. Frequently when counseling men concerning pornography, I pray with them and ask God to cause them to see the girls as He sees them. On more than one occasion I have had these men return to me and tell me stories of being tempted…opening the magazines and seeing little girls crying for daddy's approval and help.
- **HEARING** – How many of you have songs that were special to you years ago, and every time you hear them, a particular feeling returns? This is a form of a *soul-tie*.
- **TASTING** – In Genesis 2:9 in the Garden of Eden, the tree was said to be "pleasing to the sight and good for food." Remember that normal natural senses are not hurtful in and of themselves. The problem comes when these senses trigger a response that causes us to substitute for God's grace in our life.
- **SMELLING** – One of the most effective deterrents is repulsive smells. At the first church that I pastored, I had a unique problem of counseling several men that were forward observers in Viet Nam. On more than one occasion they shared the terrible smell of burning flesh and how they could not even barbecue in any longer.

I had a former staff member that served in Viet Nam. One day we took his car into a mechanic. Before we got through the door, he turned and said to me in a panicking voice, "I have to get out of here." He grabbed his nose and ran. Later when I caught up with him he told me, when he walked through the door, he smelled Viet Cong (Charlie – a slang term). Because of a traumatic experience previously, this particular smell triggered a fear reaction.

One of the greatest by-products of "Soul-ties" is what is known as "spiritual adultery." Spiritual adultery occurs whenever *you give place to another, which exceeds the intimacy you have with the one God has designed to meet your needs.*

Spiritual adultery bears this distinctive mark, it is always at first unintentional.

Spiritual Adultery usually occurs in *deficits*. When there is an absence of affection in a relationship, it tends to open the heart to search out and find this needed affection. Remember affection has **five basic avenues**: *touching, spending quality time, encouragement, listening, and the giving of gifts*, which have value to the recipient. So, when a man or woman is void of affection, their heart tends to wander. In addition, this *wandering heart* is in a perilous position, with a potential to be snared by the affections of another.

Remember, a heart void of affection will *wander, pervert*, or *become hard*. Also remember, spiritual adultery always begins unintentionally…a friend who understands…who make you feel valuable and important…who listens…it always feels so right!

So how do you avoid this dreaded Spiritual Adultery?

Don't get isolated – don't have as your basic *"modus operandi"* withdrawal. Learn to talk things out. Communicate.

Be Aware of the Symptoms

- A tendency to share private intimate matters with friends before your spouse
- Spending large amounts of time with one member of the opposite sex – even sometimes inventing reasons to work alongside that person
- Finding more delight in being with some other person than with your spouse
- Begin to think that this person understands you better than your spouse
- Unwillingness to hear the warnings of others – you are so certain that this is a platonic relationship
- Beware of the youthful "high" when you are around this person

- Begin to recognize romantic feelings – you try at first to transfer them to your spouse thinking yourself a better lover at home
- Aggressive defensiveness – becomes more and more hostile when people warn you
- Watch out for divisiveness

Find a good small group to help process these things – or a stronger brother / sister for accountability

What do you do if you have fallen? What do you do if you find yourself already in the web of a Soul Tie… especially that of spiritual adultery?

You must make a choice to release the other person. This involves both physical and emotional detachment. This means, a willingness to never see the other again. The first response is always, "we can work this out."

Have others join you and lay hands on you in praying the **soul ties to be disconnected.**

Address the dysfunction between you and your spouse. Frequently some type of counseling is helpful with this stage.

Heart Writing

How many of you know the passage about "where the Spirit of the Lord is there is Liberty?" (2Cor. 3:17)… then v.18 says, "… we are being transformed into the same image from glory to glory…" Now note that the context of these famous verses is that of *"Heart Writing."*

2 Cor.3:3 says, "written not with ink, but with the Spirit of the living God, not on tablets of stone, but on tablets of human hearts." Therefore, what is written on our hearts determines our actions, responses, and behavior. What is written on your heart? How did it get there?

Now there is an important concept here that we need to grasp: if God can write on our hearts, others can also write on our hearts.

What or **who** writes on our hearts? Let me give you several writing tools for our hearts:

1. **Traumatic events** reinforced by secondary experiences. For example, many who have been abused have hearts that have been written on by the trauma they experienced. Abuse always writes things like, "You deserved it." "You did something wrong." "You ought to be ashamed." This type of trauma always writes that which devalue and demean us. These are not so much words that we read with our eyes and understand with our minds... but remember these are written on the heart... so they are *more felt rather than read*. These writings are like "cues" that signal a particular type of behavior. Other traumas write their own particular "behavior cues."

2. **Judgments resulting in vows & curses** – Mt.7: 1 says, *"Do not judge so that you will not be judged. "For in the way you judge, you will be judged; and by your standard of measure, it will be measured to you."*

The *Message* says these verses this way: *"Don't pick on people, jump on their failures, criticize their faults—unless, of course, you want the same treatment. (2) That critical spirit has a way of boomeranging."*

Now *judgments* have two stepchildren: *vows* (an inward determination) and *curses* (an outward expression). Probably the most frequent judgment is "I will never treat my children the way my parents treated me." Another is, "I will never marry anyone like my father." "I will never marry anyone like my mother."

These judgments write on the heart, that which ensures the exact opposite behavior.

Therefore, you get married. Your first years are wonderful. Then a few years into the marriage you begin to fight and argue. Soon the arguments escalate. Then finally one day, in the midst of the argument, out of your mouth comes the statement: "You are just like my father!" "You are just like my mother!" The very behavior you detested is that which you now have.

Now you may have *a question about judgments*: "What if the individual has been hurt by the parent and this assessment or evaluation is simply a defensive step prior to setting boundaries?" There is a step prior to setting a boundary that is necessary. It is necessary to *evaluate and determine the source and effect of behaviors that are destructive* in order to properly set a boundary. But even then the "discernment" and "information" used to make this determination is not released outside your realm of authority and responsibility. There are *two good "determiners" that will help you discern whether or not you have made a judgment*:

(1) *Do you feel pain when you think about that person, circumstance or event?* If you do, chances are that you were wounded and most likely that wound has precipitated a judgment.

(2) *Is your "discernment" or "information" which is used to make this determination attached to a negative or positive thought or feeling?* If it is attached to a negative thought or feeling chances are that you have made a judgment. For example, do you treat your children the way you do because you have a conviction of a principle or truth in scripture? Or, do you treat you children the way you do because you have a bad memory of a time your parents treated you the opposite? The former is attached to positive "information" (truth of scripture) while the other is attached to "negative" information (the way your parents treated you) which is most likely a judgment.

3. *Choices reinforced by repetitious behavior.* When you make choices, not the "one-time" choice, but rather that which is reinforced by repetition, that choice will result in a type of behavior. According to the amount of repetition, that behavior may be a simple habit or an entrenched destructive behavior.

Remember the later part of Mt.7: 2, *"by your standard of measure, it will be measured to you."* The word *"measure"* denotes an *"amount"* ... *a frequency of repetition*.

The inevitable question is: How many times can you make a bad decision and it not affect your behavior? The answer is, I don't know... so if you can, stop it. If you cannot stop the negative decision making, get some help.

Frequently through repetition, this wrong choice is reinforced by external stimuli and an area of our soul: mind, will or emotions. When this happens the stimuli (five senses: hearing, feeling, smelling, tasting, or touching) from a person, place or thing, gets attached to an area of the soul (mental, emotional or volitional faculty); and that area of soul gets attached to the behavior. Until these attachments are separated, the destructive behavior will continue to be prompted by these *stimuli*.

4. *What the Holy Spirit "is saying."* The most productive form of *Heart Writing* is that done by God. This writing may be done through a softly spoken word into your heart or through the voice of a friend or even a radio song. The instrument of the voice of God may be many and varied... even a donkey! The idea is that what is written is according to His character... according to His heart... according to His Word.

Again, like any development of behavior, when the word is received, there will be some sort of action or response that will begin to "activate" that prompting to a certain behavior. Therefore, you will have to *choose* to engage that particular *response*. In addition, as you walk out that *response*, repetition will again convert the initial *response* to an entrenched *behavior*.

Different Types of Hearts

Now there are different types of hearts upon which we write. The parable of the sower and the seed speaks about three types of hearts:

Luke 5 "A farmer went out to sow his seed. Some of it fell on the road; it was tramped down and the birds ate it. 6 Other seed fell in the gravel; it sprouted, but withered because it didn't have good roots. 7 Other seed fell in the weeds; the weeds grew with it and strangled it. 8 Other seed fell in rich earth and produced a bumper crop. 9 His disciples asked, "Why did you tell this story?" 10 He said, "You've been given insight into God's kingdom—you know how it works. There are others who need stories. However, even with stories some of them aren't going to get it: Their eyes are open but don't see a thing, Their ears are open but don't hear a thing. 11 "This story is about some of those people. The seed is the Word of God. 12 The seeds on the road are those who hear the Word, but no sooner do they hear it than the Devil snatches it from them so they won't believe and be saved. 13 "The seeds in the gravel are those who hear with enthusiasm, but the enthusiasm doesn't go very deep. It's only another fad, and the moment there's trouble it's gone. 14 "And the seed that fell in the weeds—well, these are the ones who hear, but then the seed is crowded out and nothing comes of it as they go about their lives worrying about tomorrow, making money, and having fun. 15 "But the seed in the good earth—these are the good-hearts who seize the Word and hold on no matter what, sticking with it until there's a harvest. (From *The Message*)

- *(1) Unprepared Heart* - In the story this heart is actually a road…not exactly the place you should be planting a crop. Some people have not come to the place where their hearts have been prepared… where they have given any thought to God and His purposes in their lives. So when God speaks, **they don't have a paradigm to know that it is God**, rather than their own thoughts
- *(2) Hard Hearts* - these hearts are **not able to respond** to God's word. Due to **repeated rejection** of God's word…either because of already existing wounds, overriding needs or simple choices, the heart has become hard (unable to respond). The result is that the seed, the right *cue*, is not able to enter the heart to *prompt* the right behavior.
- *(3) Thorny Hearts* – These hearts are those that have other wounds and behaviors acting against the "behavior" part. They hear the *prompt* from God, they receive the prompt, but before it can produce the proper behavior, the prompt is

over-ridden by other needs. This produces what is known as ***need-oriented behavior***.

(4) Good Hearts – this is a heart that has three notable characteristics:
- ***Honesty*** – quality, condition or characteristic of being fair, just, truthful, candor
- ***Good*** - generous & kind - grace centered
- ***Perseverance*** - until behavior is produced

The Results of Heart Writing

(1) ***Definitions which affect our understanding*** - For example, one heart writing that results from a girl being abused by a man is 'all men are dogs that will only use and abuse you." It is a well-proven statistic, that women that have been abused frequently struggle with their beliefs about men in general. These beliefs continue for the remainder of their lives... unless there is an intervention.

Another common *heart writing* that is the result of a dominating mother is, "Strong women are Jezebels." Again, this writing affects the ongoing beliefs and understanding about strong women in general.

(2) ***Definitions that define our person*** - Especially when severe trauma like abuse is evident, whether emotional abuse, physical abuse or verbal abuse, abuse results in a ***redefinition of our person.*** Severe trauma's often affect our *Core Identity*. In such a case as abuse, such writing results in a loss of value, feeling of unworthiness, and feelings of inadequacy and shame.

(3) ***Conclusions that affect our perceptions*** - Sometimes the *heart writing* results in a destructive conclusion. Here are a few destructive conclusions: "Since I was hurt by a man, if I trust men, I will be used and hurt." "Since I have experienced others letting me down and not fulfilling my expectations, if I want the job done right, I must do it myself." "Since I have had bad past experiences when I have told others my problems, if I open up, it will be thrown back in my face later." These conclusions become cues to difficult non-trusting behaviors.

Erasing Wrong Heart Writing

When we find that the events of our past or our judgments have written negative and destructive "prompts" on our hearts, we have to take steps to *erase* the negatives on our heart and replace them with positive, constructive prompts.

1.*The first step is to identify the destructive behavior.* This is most frequently the easiest step to a trained counselor, or even a close family member. However, if the behavior is being hidden by a false identity, this may be somewhat difficult. If the behavior is covered by denial, it may be difficult to discover.

2.The second step is the *identification of the lie that is written on the heart.* This step is best begun with the three general lies found in Genesis 3 and then evolved to the point of the behavior dysfunction. The three general lies are: (1) God does not care about me, (2) Life is unfair (3) I am deformed... I am lacking... God says I am in His image, but I am not... something is wrong with me. After discerning the general lie, work towards the more specific lie... which the patient most frequently will recognize or even know.

For example: Through years of parental comparison of one sibling with another, one sibling receives the general lie... "You are lacking... something is wrong with you otherwise you would be able to be like you brother/sister." After talking with the patient about his feelings when around the sibling, you are usually able to discover the specific lie, "you will never succeed... you will be a failure." This lie, written into the heart has the ability to communicate a "failure mentality" every time the individual encounters the pressure of a competition. Therefore, when the opportunity for a job promotion occurs, the "failure mentality" takes over and the individual is defeated before he begins... all because of something written on his heart many years before.

Sometimes the *heart writing* is passed down from a *previous generation* in the form of an *iniquity*. This *iniquity* is a *propensity* toward a certain type of behavior. *If the behavior is in fact "transgenerational", the connection between the iniquity and the heart must be separated for the changed behavior to be lasting.*

3. The *lie is replaced with the truth*. This step is most frequently combined with a type of heart healing referred to as "*inner healing*." This process is accomplished through prayer and is necessary for the trauma to be rendered ineffective. The truth that replaces the lie is best "personalized" as it is spoken to the patient. The use of the *name* and *any specific situations* in speaking the "*truth*" is important. This truth, like the lie, needs *repetition as reinforcement*. At the onset, daily "confession" of this truth is a helpful reminder.

4. *Soul-ties* frequently hinder the healing process. When an area of the soul (mind, will, or emotions) is sufficiently attached to a stimuli (anything sensory…especially involving a relationship), that *tie* between the soul and the stimuli must be separated. Until that separation occurs, whenever a sensory stimuli is encountered, the *lie* written in the heart is activated and the destructive behavior reoccurs. Therefore, for complete healing to occur, the *soul-tie must be separated*.

5. As with any destructive behavior, *change involves the entire person… body, soul and spirit*. The heart has to desire to be changed. This part of the process is frequently called "*repentance*" … which literally means, "to change how you perceive things." Once the decision is made and the desire to change is expressed through "*confession*" the rest of the *changing process* can take place. If the patient does not desire change, the rest of the *ministry* will not be effective.

After change has been affected, repetition of the new behavior will reinforce and ensure it's lasting effect.

Lost Places of Your Soul

⇜🪷⇝

I received a telephone call from a young couple asking if they could come in for a bit of newly wed counseling. I scheduled them in for later that afternoon. Now when I think of newly-weds, I usually consider communication skills, conflict resolution, etc. But that afternoon, I had a most perplexing conversation.

The couple was a sharp couple, with hearts for God. But what I was about to hear, I was not prepared for. After the normal cordialities, I asked, "tell why you are here." The wife dropped her head, and the husband began to explain.

They had been married only 3 months, and were having a very difficult time in their physical relationship. In fact, when they would begin to share any level of physical intimacy... even prolonged kissing, she would get nauseous and develop headaches. I asked if she had been to a doctor for a physical. She replied that she had a physical just prior to their wedding. She then told me, "I have about a four to five year period when I was young, that I cannot clearly remember. I look at our family album and it looks familiar, but I can't recall the events, yet I see myself in the pictures."

For decades psychologists, psychiatrists, and counselors of all types have struggled with the issue of lost or repressed memory. Some things are forgotten usually because they are not "attached" sufficiently simply because they are not that important... not priority. Other things are referred to as ***repressed memory*** or in more clinical terms, *"traumatic amnesia."* I call these ***"lost places of your soul."***

Some of the most stereotypical causes of "lost places of your Soul" (repressed memories) are such things as physical abuse... usually that which would have a large amount of shame attached to it like child pornography or the witness of a death or other horrific event (especially of one you know or one who is close to you).

Understand Your Memory

There are two basic parts to your memory: **storage** and **retrieval**.

Storage has two parts:

- Short term storage is basically "sensory" oriented. It receives the stimuli. This is where "arousal" takes place. "Stimuli" received continues its journey through *meditation.*
- The conversion from *short-term* memory to *long-term* memory involves *reinforcement.* It is within *reinforcement* that *attachment & retrieval* occur:
- *Fantasy* is where we attach the stimuli to a visual picture within our minds. This aids us in future retrievals.
- *Personalizing (enactment)* is where acting out the feelings come in. You don't just feel anger, you stand and yell and shake your fist.
- *Repetition* (frequency of use) is where habits are developed. Repetition entrenches the mental picture or the destructive behavior.
- *Attachment* is where you attach the mental picture or feeling with something familiar. In the case of traumatic events this attachment is difficult or impossible.

So when we have a "lost place of the soul" it is frequently a case of a trauma that is not attached to that which is familiar and already stored in the memory.

How do we "lose places" of our soul?

Some "places" are lost due to **lack of "attachment" or "reinforcement."** Simply put, they were not important at the time and did not leave an "impression," therefore they are forgotten.

Other "places" are **"hidden" away.** This is **a type of will-full repression**. For example, my father's generation held to a type of premise that men do not express emotion. Due to such issues as World-war One and World-war two, etc., emotions in these circumstances were seen to be more of a hindrance rather than a help, therefore the entire culture repressed the "feeling" aspect and later in life find themselves unable to "get in touch" with many areas of emotions.

Other "places" are lost due to traumatic encounters. For example, when our bodies encounter pain, they have what is commonly referred to as a *"pain threshold"*. This *"pain threshold"* speaks of the maximum level of pain that we can endure... after which, we "pass out." What is happens in the physical realm is similar to what happens emotionally when we are faced with a *shocking traumatic event?* Some of these traumas might be physical abuse as a child, viewing the death of a loved one, witnessing the extreme pain of a loved one, etc.

How do we discover the lost places?

Lost places usually surface when contingent emotions are "bumped." For example, if I saw someone murdered by being pushed off a cliff, I might "repress" that memory as an emotional defensive measure. I might also experience extreme nausea whenever I get near a high place, especially a cliff.

Lost places are also discovered when there are abnormal emotional restraints or behaviors without any apparent cause. Remember the example I began this talk with of the young newly-wed who could not engage her husband with emotional intimacy.

Some are more obvious... the person simply cannot remember sections of time during their life.

Once "lost places" are suspect, there are several tools to aid in recovering these lost places.

Aid in Recovering "Lost Places"

Because I deal with distinctively **Christ-O-therapy**, there are several **psychotherapy techniques** that I am not comfortable with that may be used by other therapists.

Some commonly used Techniques of Psychologists

- *Guided Imagery* in which patients imagine scenarios described by the therapist... a type of visualization where you try to imagine what happened. This tends to produce false memories.
- *Suggesting false memories* - Memory errors are not random. What is recalled depends on current beliefs, inferences, guesses, expectancies, and suggestions. People can clearly be led by suggestions to integrate a fabricated event into their personal histories.

In fact, this *"false memory syndrome"* has become such an issue with the courts that there is actually a foundation called "False Memory Syndrome Foundation," and is an advocacy group for families affected by false-memory syndrome. At the time of this writing, it has researched 105 court cases involving repressed memory: One was dropped, 42 settled out of court, 53 are pending and nine went to trial.

> I read the story of Suzanne Hughes of Northern Virginia, 31, who says she was sexually abused as a child but never repressed the memory. At age 25, Hughes was suffering from postpartum depression when she lost her firstborn child to a congenital defect.
>
> "When my oldest died it broke my heart," Hughes recalls. "I was crying all the time, I had mood swings and I started drinking." When she stopped imbibing (to drink something,

especially like alcohol), Hughes says she was haunted by constantly recurring memories of the sexual abuse she had suffered.

In 1990 Hughes admitted herself to a hospital, because of an eating disorder, depression and a history of being sexually abused. Eventually she "remembered" her past, which involved abuse and other difficulties. Later to find she was simply suffering from post-partum depression... and within 18-months of the birth, she died.

- *Hypnosis* - Many therapists endorse popular yet mistaken beliefs about hypnosis. Yapko's (1994) survey revealed that 47 percent of a sample composed of professionals had greater faith in the accuracy of hypnotic than non-hypnotic memories, 54 percent believed to some degree that hypnosis is effective for recovering memories as far back as birth.

Most adults' earliest reported memories date back to between 36 and 60 months of age. The average age of the initial reported memory was 3.7 years: Only 11 percent of individuals reported memories at or before age 24 months, and 3 percent reported a memory from age 12 months or younger.

From a Christian perspective, I am not comfortable with this technique due to the influence of the demonic. It is interesting to me that most of the realm of psychology notes the difficulties with satanic rituals, yet they do not factor in the demonic into their techniques of therapy.

- *Age-regression* - involves "regressing" a person back through time to an earlier life period. Subjects are typically asked to mentally recreate events that occurred at successively earlier periods in life, or to focus on a particular event at a specific age, with suggestions to fully relive the event.
- *Symptom Interpretation* - Therapists often inform suspected abuse victims that their symptoms suggest

a history of abuse (Blume 1990, Fredrickson 1992). Examples of symptom interpretation can be found in many popular psychology and self-help sources (e.g., Bass and Davis 1992). Some popular self-help books on the topic of incest include lists of symptoms (e.g., "Do you use work or achievements to compensate for inadequate feelings in other parts of your life?") that are presented as possible or probable correlates of childhood incest.
- ***Dream Interpretation*** - Viewed by Freud as the "royal road to the unconscious," dreams have been used to provide a window on past experiences, including repressed traumatic events.
- ***Bibliotherapy*** - Many therapists prescribe "survivor books" or self-help books written specifically for survivors of childhood abuse to provide "confirmation" that the individual's symptoms are due to past abuse and to provide a means of gaining access to memories. The books typically provide stories of other survivors' struggles, as well as potential support for actual abuse survivors

Some key aids to recovering Lost Places in your Soul

A desire to discover and recover – where there is a resistance, there is usually great difficulty and even detriment in pursuing a recovery process.

Progressive Healing – as contiguous parts of the soul are healing from their wounds, their healing tends to "bump" hidden and lost areas. Work on the areas that you are aware of, and trust God to bring the rest to light at the appropriate time. Remember 1Jn.1: 7 encourages us to "**walk in the light as He is in the light and we have fellowship (intimate relationship) with one another...**" Keep walking in what you know to do!

Snapshots of the past – frequently in Christ-O-therapy, the use of words of knowledge and words of wisdom provide a "snapshot" of the past. A key bit of information that "bumps" the memory.

Regressive Prayers – these are Spirit-led prayers that are prayed, praying back through specific ages and events in the person's life, without their cognitive contribution.

Dream Interpretation – frequently dreams are used by God to reveal hidden things. There are two basic approaches to **Dream Interpretation.** The first is that dreams represent "exact replicas" of traumatic experiences. The second is that dreams are a vehicle by which "buried memories of abuse intrude into ... consciousness".

Most Christians think of **dream interpretation** as that which speaks about the future... but remember in the Spirit realm time is continuous... in other words, it is a line that goes both forward and backward... it is the picture of **infinity**. Some dreams point forward, but other dreams point to today... to help us integrate our experiences into our emotions. Other dreams point to our past, helping us unlock doors where emotions and memories have been hidden and to shine a light on areas of our soul which have been lost.

Counseling with Children

The pattern for ministering to children is similar to that of adults; however, there are some additional elements to be considered. Children are not adults. They don't have the same measure of control over their own lives that adults have, and they have different perspectives because there are many things they have not learned about living. Children will not be able to tell us as much about their problems, especially if they are small children. Therefore, we minister to children from a little different perspective.

There are three primary objectives in ministering to children. The first is the same as in all adult counseling, to untangled entrenched behaviors. When we minister to a child, we not only have the objective of helping the child to freedom, but also his parents and the entire household. We are trying to put that family in order. The enemy does not want us to do that, but don't be intimidated by what the enemy doesn't like. Remember that we have authority over him.

The second objective is found in Malachi 4:5,6 "...And he will turn the hearts of the fathers to the children, and the hearts of the children to their fathers..."

The second purpose is to restore right order and honor within the family, to turn the hearts of the fathers to the children and the children to the fathers. Parents must always be honored and built up in front of their children. The children need to understand that their parents are their covering. When we minister to children the parents should always be present and should be treated with great honor and respect.

The third purpose is to show the character of God to that child. We must be positive and supportive, helping the child feel good about himself, about what is happening, and to be glad to receive ministry.

Pray in accordance to these purposes, so that the atmosphere of any counseling session with children will be one that is positive and uplifting. It should make both the parents and the children feel good about what takes place.

Jesus is shown in a classic ministry session for children in Mark 9:17-19. "...I asked your disciples to drive out the spirit, but they could not." Here the man brought his son to the disciples for ministry, and they failed to get the job done.

Mark 9:20-21 "Jesus asked the boy's father, 'How long has he been like this?'" Notice that even Jesus asked questions. He asked the father how long this had been happening. This was a very short interview, but it was a stage of inquiry. In addition, He asked the father. He honored the father.

Mark 9:22-24 "Help me overcome my unbelief!" He strengthens the father's belief. A major part of the ministry to children is ministry to their parents.

Mark 9:25 "I command you, come out of him and never enter him again." Then He did the ministry. He delivered the child. This is the only place in the Bible that the Lord commands a demon not to enter ever again.

Now look at something in the same story in Luke 9:42. "...And deliver him back to his father." When you minister to children, always release them back to the parents. Always remember that the parents are the *primary caregiver* for that child.

The preparation for a counseling session with children is much the same as that for adults. We need the same time in intercession, the same time to let God show us our own heart as well as the situation with the family to whom we will minister.

This ministry session is a little different in that there should be three people to minister instead of just two. That is because there may be a time that the child will be taken to a separate place while the team talks to the parents. The third person will take care of the child. There should always be someone with the child.

In the beginning of the session, the parents and the children will be together. It is important to establish the confidence of both the parents and the child. The ministry team will have pencils and paper to take notes. One method to make the child more at ease is to give him a pencil and paper so he can draw pictures. Another technique is to discreetly ask the parents if it is all right to give the child a mint. By asking the parents if it is all right, we show our respect for their authority in the child's life. By giving the child a small treat, we help establish a relationship with the child.

The team will ask questions to try to locate wounds in the child. Don't ask questions that would imply any guilt on the part of the parents. You can ask about times when peers or teachers have said things that hurt.

Many times as we deal with hurts or shame that others have caused, the parents will begin to see areas where they have hurt their children. Watch for shame and give love and acceptance to break the shame as soon as it comes. Watch the child's eyes. Many times a child will not be able to express what is bothering him, but his eyes will be very revealing. Sometimes drawing out a situation with crayons is helpful for children. Playing with dolls or other props can also provide the child a means of expressions a situation or traumatic event.

When we feel we have sufficient understanding with the child present, we may send the child out with the third person on the ministry team. This person will primarily be taking care of the child. All therapy to the child will take place in the presence of the parents. When the child is gone, the parents can be dealt with like a regular counseling session. Follow the same lines as a normal counseling session. If the parents are antagonistic to the things of the Lord, it may be difficult to continue to minister to the child.

However, if the parents, particularly the father is open to spiritual things the ministry will be easier. It may be the way to show him the power of God and bring him into that relationship with Christ.

Talk to them about what you sense the problem areas are and how these things affect the child. You may ask if they have ever hurt their child, called them names, spoken word curses over them, etc. During separate times with the parents only, you can teach them about *discipline with dignity*, and other ways to communicate value to their children.

You will probably find areas where they need personal counseling. Don't try to do it in this session. Ask if they are open to counseling at a future time. During this session, we are only trying to provide a support and help for the child. We are really only applying a band-aid until we can minister in-depth to the parents.

Then, bring the child back with the parents. If the team needs to momentarily leave the room to discuss strategy, they should do so at this time. It is very important to discern if the family should be left alone or if one of the counselors should stay with them to maintain peace and right atmosphere. Fear can move in quickly.

When the counseling plan is formed, ministry will be done with the child along with the parents. Explain to the child that his parents are going to pray for him because they have the place of authority over his life. This honors the parents, and it also teaches the parents how to pray for their children and deal with the problems on an ongoing basis. You will instruct the father how to pray. He will repeat after you, but he will do the praying.

Most of the time the child will not need to confess sin or do much praying himself. That is because the majority of the problems in children are simply a response to their needs. Be careful to handle the child in a way to be positive and supportive. Do not allow shame. Always be reinforcing and encouraging to add value to their life.

Parental instructions are always important. After the counseling session, have a short debriefing time with the parents so they can ask questions.

Symptoms of Child Abuse

Virtually every state has a child abuse reporting law requiring anyone who comes into contact with children in the course of their employment or in the practice of their counseling to report child abuse and neglect. Once a counselor suspects abuse or neglect, they should be careful to record, document and then report the finding. Remember the "good faith" provision in child abuse statutes protects mandated reporters from legal prosecution if the report turns out to be unfounded.

According to David Sandberg (Sandberg, Crabbs, & Crabbs, 1988), a noted attorney who specializes in children's issues, several conditions are ***not necessary*** for a child abuse report to be filed.

1. The reporter does not have to "prove" that child abuse has occurred but need only to "suspect" that it has occurred.
2. The child does not have to acknowledge that abuse is occurring as a precondition for reporting.
3. The *"child protective services"* bears the responsibility for determining whether there is enough evidence to warrant an investigation.

To motivate the counselors to notify the appropriate authorities of suspected abuse, many states have failure-to-report statutes in their child abuse law that include the risk of prosecution and the fines that can be levied.

Some abused children appear to live normally, whereas others, feeling unloved and unwanted, are on the brink of suicide. Because children can be abused and neglected in a variety of ways and to varying degrees, it is especially important for counselors to be aware of some of the contradictions in the child's behavior.

Only a few clear-cut characteristics have emerged to differentiate neglect and abuse (Kempe & Kempe, 1978; Fontana, 1984; Goldstein, 1987; Helfer & Kempe, 1987; Herman-Giddens, 1984; National Research Council, 1993).

Common Signs of Abuse and Neglect

1. **Injuries that cannot be explained as accidental.** A pattern of bruises, cuts, burns or other injuries; for example, the imprint of a steam iron on the upper leg, burns on the small of the back, or lacerations made by a lamp cord. Others signs are frequent and repeated injuries in various stages of healing. Genital or rectal tears, pain, bleeding, infection, or sexually transmitted diseases in the mouth, vagina, or anus are signs of sexual abuse. Denial of medical treatment or long delays in seeking help for the child are often a part of the pattern of abuse.
2. **Lack of trust.** Often the victim of inconsistent parental punishment, deceit, and broken promises, the abused child learns that it is unwise to trust others.
3. **Fearful, shy, and withdrawn behavior.** Hyper-vigilant and always alert to danger, the child avoids conflict (and punishment) by being compliant and submissive.
4. **Aggressive, acting-out behavior.** The child moves constantly and is often unable to sit still or attend. He or she seems unaffected by disapproval and is more concerned with avoiding punishment than avoiding wrongdoing. This may lead to delinquent behavior.
5. **Extreme difficulty in recognizing and verbalizing feelings.** The child needs encouragement to express both negative (fear, hurt, loneliness) and positive (joy, pleasure) emotions. Some children do not cry even when they are in pain; others cry easily.
6. **Feelings of profound sadness.** Crying spells, sleep disturbances, changes in eating habits, and avoiding contact with others are common signs. The child may evidence self-destructive behavior such as head banging, scratching, cutting, or hair pulling. Some older abused children think about committing suicide.
7. **Excessive fears, sleep disturbances, and regressive behavior.** The child may fear going to bed, have nightmares, want the light on, wake up in the middle of the night, and fear sleeping alone. These behaviors may be accompanied by renewed fears

of the dark or of monsters in the closet. The child may regress and begin wetting the bed again or sucking the thumb. These responses are often associated with sexual molestation of children.
8. **Poor self-esteem.** Abused children tend to see themselves as "stupid," "bad," or "unlovable." Some abused and neglected children are labeled as "lazy" by their teachers because of their inability to concentrate and because they are under-achievers. Sexually abused children may see themselves as "dirty."
9. **Incapable of playing acceptably with other children.** Abused and neglected children have difficulty having fun. They may avoid activities with peers such as sports and gym class. Sexually abused children may avoid playing with peers for they fear that others can tell they are abused just by looking at them.
10. **Persistent and inappropriate sexual play with self and peers.** This includes sexually aggressive behavior towards others, excessive masturbation, and excessive sexual curiosity, which are commonly seen in sexually abused children. The have sexual knowledge that is beyond their developmental level: for example, a 3-year old simulates intercourse during doll play.
11. **Adult-like behavior.** Neglected children, who must care for their entire families at young ages, or children who are sexually abused often act "grown up." Adult-like in their speech and behavior, these children have little understanding of the meaning and consequences of adult behaviors. Older abused children model adult behavior and may abuse younger, weaker children or severely punish children left in their care.
12. **School attendance.** Some abused children have few absences, arrive early, and find excuses not to go home. Others are frequently kept home to care for younger children, to wait for bruises to heal, or to be sexually available to a male caretaker while the mother is working.
13. **Evidence of care.** Poor hygiene, lack of preventive health care (teeth decayed) undernourished (always asking for food) inappropriately dressed for the weather (no coat in winter), or lack of supervision after school and in the evening (home alone or roaming the streets at night) may be signs of abuse or neglect.

In addition, the child may wear long sleeves in summer to hide bruises. Sexually abused children may bath excessively or not at all, because some children hope that being dirty and unattractive will stop the abuse.

Reporting child abuse is a serious responsibility that cannot be taken lightly. The counselor must decide whether the child is being abused on the basis of his or her observation of the child's physical condition, mood, and affect, as well as the child's direct and indirect verbal and nonverbal cues.

Reporting child abuse always puts the child at risk, and it has serious consequences for the counselor's relationship to the child. Because a terrible secret has been revealed, they may feel betrayed by the counselor, or the family may retaliate against the child if he or she remains in the home. This is why follow-up and careful monitoring of abusive situations is essential. Although it may not be possible, the counselor needs to attempt to maintain contact with the child and his or her family.

Practical Suggestions

- Remember that a secret told to just one person isn't a secret anymore. Guard clients' confidence except when they must be broken in cases involving danger to self and others.
- If something bothers you about a particular decision or course of action and if you sense that it isn't right, legally, ethically or morally, don't do it!
- Listen to your heart... to the Holy Spirit within you, when it comes to reporting suspected child abuse. Better to report and be wrong than fail to report and be right.
- Be careful what you commit to in writing about a child in your personal notes or files. Ask yourself: Would I want someone to say this about me or about my child? Will this information harm the child (even as an adult) if it ever becomes public?
- Remember that a child's parents are partners in the counseling process. Keep the parents and the children involved in

all aspects of the decisions and provide positive feedback to both.
- The best way to avoid the possibility of lawsuits is to develop a warm relationship with counselees. Always have their best interest at heart. It is difficult to sue someone who acts in "good faith."

Understanding the Model
[Understanding Christ-O-Therapy]

⇜🙏⇝

We have talked about many aspects of destructive behavior and of counseling. Now let's look at a model for a counseling session. We need to understand that this model isn't sacred. The Holy Spirit may guide us to go other directions during the session. This is to give us a guide, so we have some structure to work within.

Presuppositions:

This model was developed in a church that was well organized and had more than sixty trained lay counselors. This model schedules multiple appointments at fixed times to allow for preparation and maximum effectiveness in counselor supervision. Counselors are supervised by a professionally trained counselor or therapist. The sessions take place in one of six counseling rooms prepared with a small table, tissues, breath mints and three chairs. One-way mirrors enable the supervisor to look into room to observe the session. The client is always positioned with their back to the door. The counselor is trained to signal a need for help from the supervisor by moving the small box of mints to the other end of the table. All session are with two counselors, one primary leading the session and a secondary observing and learning.

For example, you have sessions available on Monday evenings, Thursday evenings and Saturday mornings. Many times, we will find ourselves working in a situation that is not ideal. There will be times that we have no time to prepare. Sometimes we can set up a time to do the counseling later. Sometimes there is just no choice but to crisis-counsel immediately. In such cases the grace of God is sufficient to make up whatever we lack.

In this model *Christ-O-Therapy* attempts to cover every area of a session. When we are counseling, we may not cover every facet. We should know how to cover all aspects of a counseling session, but then we will allow the Holy Spirit to draw out what He wants covered in that particular session. So, not everything we talk about within this model goes into every session. It is just to help us organize and give us a game-plan.

We are going to break the counseling session into three parts. They are *preparation*, the *actual session*, and *post session*.

Preparation:

The first four steps of preparation are things you should always be aware of. The other three steps are preparation for a particular session.

- **Check your own emotional reserves** - Are you called to this type of ministry? If you aren't called to a counseling ministry, this type of ministry will tend to be extremely draining to the emotions.

  But whether you are called or not, understanding this material will help you understand yourself and other people better. Also, just as those who are not called to evangelism must be prepared to help people receive Jesus, those who are not called to personal ministry need to be prepared to help minister to the needs of people.
- **Be aware of your limitations**. There is such an immense need for people that can minister effectively, that you can become overloaded rapidly. You can't be effective if you

burn yourself out. Don't push yourself beyond your mental and emotional capacity. Beware of you limited knowledge and skill in working with emotional heart issues.
- **Be aware of your own heart's condition**. Check your own heart and make sure that your heart is rightly connected to God before you ever step into a counseling session. If you haven't dealt with the iniquity in your own heart, it will come against you when you get into a ministry session. It will intimidate you and attack you. It will do everything it possibly can to deter you from doing the job you are there to do.
- **Humility is essential**. Remember where our power and authority come from. Any time a person begins to think he is good at counseling and begins to trust his own ability instead of trusting God, that is when he is headed for a fall. Humility is essential.

Don't allow this to happen. At our very best, we are a channel for the Lord to use. If the Lord doesn't pour His life through us, we are nothing more than an empty pipe. We are there to help someone. Our attitude needs to be that of a servant. The power source and the glory belong to God.

Intercession is the first step

This is a very important part of ministry. When you find out that you are going to be in a counseling session, you are responsible to intercede for that person. This is where you actually begin the ministry session because many things can be taken care of in intercession. Your intercession will take three directions: for yourself, for the person to whom you are ministering and against the devil.

For yourself, ask God to show you your heart, so if there is anything out of order, you can pray to get it straightened out. Ask how you are to best serve Him in this situation. Pray for anointing. Ask that you be prepared to receive words of knowledge and prophecy. Acknowledge that without the Lord doing the job through you, you are helpless to do it.

Also make sure that you have your spiritual armor on. Check out your helmet of salvation, the breastplate of righteousness, etc. Do everything you can to be prepared in every way. Then don't worry about it. If you miss anything, God's grace will pick it up.

Ask for discernment concerning the person to whom you are ministering. Ask God to show you, through words of knowledge, or however He might choose to show you by His Spirit, what you are actually dealing with. Without His discernment you are operating in speculation, but it is amazing what you will learn if you will just ask. Sometimes the things you receive may not make any sense to you, but at some time in the ministry session you will be able to speak what God has shown you, and it will break through and help you gain ground. So be sensitive to this.

Thirdly, you are to come against the enemy. Bind what you see bound in heaven, and loose what you see loosed in heaven. Judge the enemy. You are a lawyer in the kingdom of God. You are appointed as a judge in this situation. So what you are doing is preparing your case long before you get to the ministry room. You want to bring judgment against those things that put the person in bondage.

Fasting sometimes helps

In the ninth chapter of Mark, there is an example of Jesus casting out a demon that his disciples had not been able to cast out. When they asked Him why they couldn't do it, Jesus answered, "This kind can come out by nothing but prayer and fasting." You may find that there are some situations that you will go into that will require you to fast.

Anointing

If we don't have the anointing going into a ministry session, we aren't equipped. Anointing is tied to submission to the Holy Spirit. The presence of the Holy Spirit working through us is absolutely essential. You can always tell when you are working out of your flesh, because you will be trying to get something to happen, and nothing happens. It takes the power of the Spirit to get results, to produce life. Sometimes the Holy Spirit will do things that don't make any sense to us. Don't worry about it. Submit to the Spirit of God, and let it flow. To the best of your ability, shut off your carnal mind when you go into a ministry session.

It is the anointing that breaks the yoke. It isn't us. No matter how good we are at ministry and how much experience we have had, we are still only a mouthpiece of the Holy Spirit. It is the Spirit of God that does all the work. Keep that foremost in your mind.

Keep your mind on what you are doing. You can quench the anointing in a counseling session by allowing your mind to wander to other things, like something that you need to do. You are in a battle. You can't afford to let your guard down.

Though it is a battle, our position and attitude must be that of "more than a conqueror." In Jesus, you have already won. Understand your covering and your authority. In that ministry room we are the anointed one. We are the sent ones. We are God's ambassadors. We have the authority. Our position is that of a king, while our attitude is that of a servant.

The Counseling Session

The counseling session will be divided into three parts: the **preparation**, the **interview** and the **ministry**. There are things about the *"setting"* itself that need to be right even before we begin the interview.

The Atmosphere

You, as the minister, affect the atmosphere of the session by various things. On the most basic level, your personal hygiene, appearance and habits are important. Make sure that you have brushed your teeth or whatever is necessary to avoid having offensive breath. Be aware of body odor and the way you are dressed. We are not under law as to how we dress, but if you are ministering to someone who has definite rules or ideas about what is acceptable dress, it is better not to offend him. Be aware of anything that you might do that would be distracting like popping your knuckles or playing with your pen.

There needs to be a sense of calm and order. Arrive at least 30 minutes early for the ministry session so everything can be in order with no sense of hurry or confusion. You can touch bases with your ministry partner. You may need to share what God has shown you or hear what someone else has received. You will also have time to get any notes, pencil, tissues, or other things that you want during the session. This all will be done before the person receiving ministry arrives, so that when you meet the person, there is an atmosphere of order and confidence.

The Counseling team

There should be at least two people ministering. It is best for women to minister to women and men to minister to men. One person should be appointed as the leader. That person has full authority. The other will back him up in prayer; however, often the second person will have insight into the situation that is valuable or will be called upon to take leadership for a period of time. This relationship needs to be clarified in advance so that in the ministry room there is an atmosphere of complete unity. The enemy would like nothing better than divide forces.

If, during a session, you find you aren't in agreement as to what should be done, do not discuss it in front of the person receiving counseling. Take a time out and go to a private place to work out the problem. There is nothing wrong with taking breaks to discuss strategy.

As you minister, keep the atmosphere supportive. Seek to always wear a smile. Keep eye contact. Don't judge the person. Separate the sin from the sinner. Let the love of God be released from your heart to the person.

Review the Pre-counseling Inventory

Careful examination of the *pre-counseling inventory* is essential. This will provide you a frame of reference for your original line of questioning. It will benefit you to outline your desired line of questioning prior to the initial session. As your counseling team meets prior to the counseling session, you will exchange ideas for the upcoming session. The "lead counselor" will have the final say on the direction of questioning… in fact, the "lead counselor" will be the only one asking questions. If both counselors are asking questions, it tends to give the client a feeling of be attacked, rather than supported.

The Connection

When the person who is to receive counseling arrives, put them at ease. If you are counseling someone whom you do not know, introduce yourself. Be cordial and supportive. You need to build their confidence in you. When a client first arrives, they are usually nervous and confused, even frightened. They will be looking to you for help and understanding because they probably won't have an understanding of what is going on spiritually. They need some friendly assurance that they are in the hands of someone who cares about them.

You can also help alleviate fears by explaining what you are going to do. Explain that you are going to ask some questions to get to know the person and to try to get a good understanding of their problem. After you have sufficient understanding of the situation, you will develop a *plan-of-restoration*. Explain that what they say will be kept confidential, but they need to understand that that confidentiality may not be limited to those in that room. For example, in a church, the pastor and the person in charge of ministry might need to know what goes on in the ministry session. Other people do not need to know and will not be told. Frequently a *"confidentiality agreement"* is the best way to denote the specifics of this issue of confidentiality.

Empathetic Listening

After cordialities, the introductory question of, "Why have you come?" is in order. During this time you may make notes always listening for cues to systems of destructive behavior. Be sure your body language is "attentive" and "encouraging." Listening and empathizing are essential skills when relating to others. Most of us spend 70% of the day communicating, 45% of that time listening. We all want to be listened to (but spouses talk only 10-20 minutes per day). It is insulting to be ignored or neglected. We all know what it means to listen, to really listen. It is more than hearing the words; it is truly understanding and accepting the other person's message and his/her situation and feelings. ***Empathy means understanding another person so well that you identify with him/her, you feel like he/she does***. The Indians expressed it as: "Walking a mile in another person's moccasins." It is listening so intently and identifying so closely that you experience the other person's situation, thoughts and emotions. Good counselors do this, so do good friends (Berger, 1987).

After the initial time of *empathetic listening* you will begin to target specifics areas of relationships asking *clarifying questions*. These *clarifying questions* are to search out specific areas or relationships such as the clients relationship with their father and mother, siblings, spouse, other authority figures in their lives, etc. The "pre-counseling inventory" becomes a helpful starting place for these questions.

Salvation Inventory

Throughout the interview you will be asking about relationships. The first relationship we need to know about is the person's relationship to the Lord Jesus. Therefore, our first responsibility as far as the counseling interview itself is concerned is to ensure that that person has a vital working relationship with God. Ask them to explain how they connect to God. Ask the type of question that requires an explanation, not one that can be answered with a simple "yes" or "no." In other words ask, "Tell me about your journey towards God." "Have you connected with God? How did you make that connection?" Attempt to use words that are non-religious in nature so that you will not trigger a religious response. If you received responses that are religious clichés, ask them what they mean by that.

If a person can't describe to you his relationship to God, he probably doesn't have one. Look for a witness in your spirit as to whether the person really has a connection with the Lord or not. If you are convinced the person has a vital working relationship with God, you don't have to take a lot of time on this step. If you are not, you need to present the gospel and give the person an opportunity to come to the Lord. Even if they say they are born again, but you have a check in your spirit that they may not, ask questions that clarify the object of their trust. You might ask, "Suppose you were to stand before the Lord and He were to ask you, 'why should I let you into my Kingdom?' What would you say to Him?" Remember that terminology does not equate to the validity of the experience.

Baptism Review

Assured of their connection to God, review with them the need for water baptism. You will find that everyone has iniquity that needs to be broken. The circumcision of the heart is one of the primary ways to apply that circumcision. So it is likely that sometime during the counseling session you will need to talk about baptism. You might ask, "Tell me what you understand about the spiritual importance of baptism? What were you expecting to receive when you were baptized?"

They need to understand what baptism is all about. You need to study and understand the lesson on baptism very well. Remember, in a counseling session you will probably have to do the jobs of teacher, pastor, evangelist... everything rolled into one. You can come up against all sorts of things in a counseling session, and you need to be prepared to explain and do whatever is necessary. So you need to know how to teach about and minister water baptism.

You also need to know how to do the same with the filling of the Holy Spirit. People need to be baptized in water and full of the Holy Spirit so they can receive the fullness of what is being offered.

Soul Mapping

As you are interviewing, you should begin your *soul-mapping*. This is the practical mapping of the cause and effect of the note problems.

Connection Period – This is the "acquaintance" period where you get to know them.
- **Empathetic Listening** - Remember, "They have to know how much you care, before they care how much you know."

Let them tell their story
- Keep eye contact
- Ask questions of interest & clarification
- Tri**age** – "stop the bleeding"
- Danger Zones – physical danger like abuse; emotional traumas; grief, etc.
- Need to Stabilize –

Deal with immediate crisis situations

Give at least one step of practical activation/implementation. The purpose of this step is two-fold: to give immediate "stop-gap" solutions; and to divert the internal emotional energy to external actions.

Set next appointment within 24 hrs.

Take History
- Natural – many need a physical (medical exam) – note hereditary problems with dad, mom, siblings, etc.
- Spiritual –
- Pre-counseling inventory (beginning point)
- Listen for patterns of behavior

Don't allow the person to sidetrack you into trying to evaluate the problems of somebody else's life. At this point we practice what we call *"circle therapy." "Circle Therapy"* is where you draw a circle around yourself and we will work on only that which is within the circle." Often in a situation, such as where there are marital problems, the person will want to talk about the problems of their spouse. They will want to place the blame there. Don't allow the client to be diverted from their own feelings, problems and responsibilities. Stop the person and redirect and restate your purpose in the counseling session if for him. Say you want to hear about the person himself, not his wife or her husband. What is it in him that causes him to respond as he does to the spouse? Remember, you cannot change what *you do not own*!

Look for **desire to change. *Where there is no desire to change, there is no recovery.*** Don't feel bad about sending someone home if there is no desire to change. Without desire and intention, it isn't time for ministry. ***Owning your own problems*** is the beginning of recovery.

- **Laser Inventory** – targeted *clarifying-questions* aimed at gathering insight to a pre-determined suspected area of problem.

For Example – A couple comes in with "anger" problem: **Questions might be:**

- When did you first recognize or remember anger explosions?
- Was anger part of your growing up experience?
- Pain-Anger Questions: (a) Rejection / Abuse / Abandonment / etc.
- How did that make you feel?

Identify the Roots – using a history profile inventory, you can search for various patterns of behavior. These patterns of behavior will disclose possible roots. Critical relationships, i.e. father, mother, spouse, etc., will also need to be inventoried to discover possible roots.

Identify the Lie – behind each root there is a general lie that operates (remember the three lies from "Soul Mapping, part I") After discovering the lie, replace it with truth. A process of "renewing the mind" is necessary for a complete paradigm change, especially as it pertains to changing from the **False Identity** to a **Legitimate Identity**.

Identify Value sources & Identity wounds - from where do you get your sense of value, worth, significance, belonging? These areas of wounding seem to present the most difficult of problems.

False Identity (Fig Leaf) - Expose the False Identity.

- Clearly identify the **lie** which produces the wrong identity
- Clearly identify the **Core Need** that is deficient causing the need for the false identity
- **Outline the Values and Standards that support the False Identity.** Interrupt and replace the **values** & **standards**. Remember that the "value system" has to change in order for the behavior to change on a long-term basis.

Dysfunction – "*Christ-O-Therapy*" is needed to complete the Restoration process. Besides the already mentioned facets of the Restoration process, some additional aids might include:

- Accountability – personal accountability may be needed to reinforce the weakened behavior
- Support Groups – helpful in aiding one in "processing" problems
- Personal Discipleship/Mentoring – necessary for ongoing growth and personal development.

Healing of heart / Memories / Child within – this part of "*Christ-O-Therapy*" may involve a type of "prophetic counseling" where "words of knowledge" and "words of wisdom" are instrumental. This type of counseling enables us to go into the past (memory regression) and then bring the emotions forward into the present. This is different from *Recovered Memory Therapy* in that simple *enlightenment* of the past does not bring resolution…

frequently this type of *enlightenment*, only results in more pain! There is still healing that needs to take place within the emotions. **Complete healing is usually a process involving memories, relationship deconstruction (offences, abandonment, abuse, etc.), pain resulting from the wounds received (remember wounds are based on perception, not necessarily reality), actual processing or understanding of the issue, choice to re-engage (from a basis of forgiveness), re-attachment, and refocus or redirection.**

- Remember, wounds keep roots alive

After you have finished the interview, you may want to take a break and draw aside with your intern-counselor to evaluate and discuss what you have both discerned. Together you can form the *plan of restoration*. It is possible that the counseling session will not go quite the direction that you planned, but if you are both receiving direction from the Holy Spirit, you should be able to form an effective *plan of restoration*.

Communicating the Plan-of-Restoration

Once you have developed the *Plan-of-Restoration*, it is important to communicate this said *"plan"* to the client. Communicate the plan in a *"summary"* fashion giving only the first three areas of *"attack"* that you intend to address.

Healing, Inner healing and Restoration

Replace the Lie with Truth

This healing begins with speaking the truth to replace the lies. These truths will reflect what God really feels and sees about the client. Remember, that until the *lie* is replaced by **truth**, the client will continue in his dysfunction. It is imperative to not only identify the *lie*, but to remove it and replace it with **truth**.

Disconnect the Soul-ties

At this point you begin disconnecting *soul-ties*. Remember a *"soul-tie"* is a *natural sense that triggers an old behavior pattern or feeling, thought or decision pattern*. These must be disconnected so that the mind and emotions can begin the healing process.

Healing in the Womb

In some instances in the inner healing phase of the counseling session, you even have to go back to the womb and speak to the child in that person before the person was even born. As unusual as this sounds, remember that in the spiritual realm there is no time. There are things that are spoken over a child in the womb that goes right into their spirit and stays with them. Speak acceptance to them, that they are loved, that they are received, that they were purposed to be here during this time. In all of this area, you are speaking value and love.

If there has been sexual abuse of the person, you will find an abandonment of a person's spirit. What happens is the child quenches its spirit after such an experience, so even if you are dealing with an adult, the spirit is still that of a child at the age the abuse took place. You'll find that spirit is hiding under a bed, hiding in a closet, hiding somewhere where that experience took place, and there the emotions get *stuck*... they quit maturing. Thus, you have a mature adult who has ten-year-old emotions in a particular area of life or relationship.

You lead the person into going back and in their mind's eye seeing where they left that child. They deserted that child so it wouldn't get hurt again. Have them, as an adult look at that child and speak to that child that it is safe. Have them tell the child to come out. They may have to open their arms and receive the child. In ministering, you may have to say something like, "Tell him to come on. It's okay. We'll get through the puberty and pimples and all those difficult times. We'll be okay because Daddy God is going to take care of us now." You just keep speaking kind, reassuring words until they bring that child up to its proper age and become whole where the spirit and the physical reality are together. This is a precious moment.

Forgiveness and Breaking Judgments

They may have to forgive themselves before they can do this. Another very important thing in the inner healing process is to have the person forgive his or herself. It is often easier to forgive everybody else in the world than it is to forgive us. So you have them speak forgiveness over themselves. "You are forgiven for..."

Judgments are one of the primary roots for many dysfunctions. Judgments must be recognized, owned and disconnected. This process is not difficult except where there is usually a wound. Frequently the pain of the wound will precipitate a judgment. Forgiveness is the key that unlocks the judgment but healing is the key to the wound.

- Forgiveness is a choice, not a feeling
- We don't forgive because they are worth it – we forgive because He asked us to forgive
- We do not forgive out of our own resources, but from the mercy He has given us
- We must release expectations / rights (Mt.18:27)
- Hebrews 10:18 says, "where there is forgiveness, there no longer remains any offering for sin." The word "offering" literally means "a price to be paid; something to be done." So when you say to someone, "I forgive you" you are releasing him or her from any further responsibility of response.
- Where necessary, forgive yourself.

Dealing with Entrenched Behaviors

This is where the actual deliverance takes place. We must emphasize the finished work of Jesus on the cross evidenced by the resurrection. Let the person know that the victory is theirs.

To deal with whatever area of entrenched behaviors that you have found, break judgments and vows. Break curses and any hereditary behavior. Deal with systems of behavior. It's important that they confess their sin in all the areas of behavior. Once the person has participated in the confession of the sins, pronounce forgiveness over those sins. The person needs to hear the pronouncement of forgiveness. It is at that point that the legal ground of the enemy has been broken.

Once the sin is confessed, it is forgiven, so the enemy has no more legal ground. The ruling and judgment has been made. At that point, you as their lawyer, representing the authority of Jesus Christ, tell the demonic presence to go. They no longer have authority to be there. The only authority they have to be there is if the person you are ministering to says he doesn't want them to go.

Always minister deliverance with your eyes open. Be alert to what is happening in the individual. If they are fidgety and uneasy, it is frequently because the spirits within them are getting uneasy. There is the possibility of all sorts of manifestations. The manifestations of women often come in the area of the womb. The manifestations with men will often show up in the hands, face and neck. It can happen other ways, but these are common.

Lay your hands on the place where you can see the manifestation, and you order the demonic presence to come out in the name of Jesus. He must go. You don't have to scream and yell. Your authority is in the name of Jesus and in the anointing resting on you, not in how loud you yell. Be firm in your conviction. Don't let anything intimidate you. You are the one with the authority. The destructive behavior will have to go.

When you finish with this stage, you have another step to take. Scripture tells us that once a spirit has been cast out, it wanders in dry areas. If it finds no rest, it says, "I will go back to my home." If he gets back to that former home and finds nothing occupying it, he will go and find seven spirits worse than himself and reoccupy. So the condition of the person will be worse afterward than before if that is allowed to happen. So ask God to fill all that has been emptied and vacated.

Basic Core Needs

Some people prefer to talk about core needs at this point. Others may prefer to do it as they are ministering other things. You do need to address deficient core needs sometime in the session. You need to explain what they are and the loss of identity and deception that is associated with them. They need to know who they are in Christ.

We have covered all these things, so that you can see all that may need to be dealt with in a person's life. You are not going to be able to teach and minister all these things in detail in any given session. You would be there several days, and besides the person couldn't handle it. The important thing is that you know all the teachings, all the material, and then let the Holy Spirit draw out of you what He wants done in this particular session. Many times, you are going to need more than one session with a person to minister all that is needed.

Post-Ministry

Renewal of the mind

Here you need to explain the restoration process. You may not get to this until the second or third session that you have with someone. You explain to the person that God's purpose is to see that person restored. In order to be restored, the mind must be renewed. The mind functions like a computer. It will only function with what you put in it. What you put in is what will come out. If a person has received garbage all their life in the form of guilt and condemnation, being put down by parents, friends and relatives, they will produce that kind of fruit.

In the renewing of the mind, they have to understand that they are no longer that person full of garbage. They are moving toward the things that God is calling them to, and God is going to give them a new identity. This will be accomplished by "washing them in the water of the word." Begin to release the word of God. Do not release your opinions. It is the entrance of the *"Word"* that gives light.

In renewing the mind, it is a wonderful time to aid them in developing a daily time with God. Keeping a journal of what they are hearing from God, as well as their prayers and needs is always a starting point. (We require this of each client for continuing in counseling. We ask them to bring their journal with them to each future session)

Walking free

Sometimes we take people through all this and then, in a couple of months, they come back for the same thing. To avoid this, they will have to change their life patterns. They must be convinced that they have to be separated from the world. They have to separate themselves from the life-style they have been practicing. If someone is trying to quit drinking, they can't spend their time in a bar. This basically holds true in the area of friends, old relationships. They need to move on to a new set of relationships, people who will not pull them back into old patterns.

Walking free also requires ***self-discipline***. It requires that we exercise authority over our thought-life. There is nothing the enemy likes better than to isolate us and start playing with our minds. We have to instruct them how to "take those thoughts captive to the obedience of Christ." We must be aware of the traffic that is going through our brain. Challenge that which is not of God. Take authority over it.

Resisting the enemy

Walking free and resisting the enemy are alike, but they do have subtle differences. Resisting the enemy requires prayer and constant connection with God. Remember there is life in the presence of God, death and darkness outside His presence.

People must understand that they are going to encounter tests. Usually those tests start right away. We will be tested continually until we are stable in that area of our life.

The person needs to understand that they will fail and fall. Everyone does. We need to understand that when we miss it, we must own the problem, we can change our perception, get back up, and go on. The failing and falling will diminish as we grow. The important thing is that we change how we think about the problem, get up and go again. Don't give up. Keep on adjusting our *"processing"* and keep on practicing all that has been given to help us stand. It is through perseverance that character is built to overcome. There will come a time when that area is not longer a result of discipline, but rather a fruit of their lifestyle.

Finally in resisting the enemy, depression results by loss of purpose. We need to have a vision of the person that God has called us to be and hang onto that vision. Frequently this is aided by being part of a small group or a support group.

Accountability

This is personal responsibility. We must understand that the things that happen to us are our responsibility. Perhaps we have a lot of iniquity and curses that came down from previous generations; nevertheless, ultimately it is our responsibility. We must face the issue that we are responsible for what happens to our life from this moment on and not try to shift the blame to any other person or thing.

Secondly, we must be open to examination. We must be willing for others to tell us when they see a problem.

Frequently the client would like to be accountable to the counselor. This is rarely effective. Support groups are a great help in this area. If a support group is not available, you need to instruct the client to find a person or two who will hold them accountable. On many occasions, that "other person" will begin to attend future counseling sessions along with the client.

Covering

The person needs to be planted in a good church. They need to be a part of a body where they can be held accountable and where people will care for them. They need to be where they can become grounded in the word of God, involved in a small group, and learn how to stand for themselves. When the client is associated with another church, we allow only an initial visit prior to requiring written permission from their pastor. This written permission also grants us permission to debrief their pastor on the counseling session. On some occasions, the pastor will then accompany them to the counseling session.

Report and Debriefing

After the counseling session, a brief report is filled out and filed. This report notes the client's particulars and the general highlights of the counseling session. After the written report is filed, the attending supervisor prays for each counselor. This is a prayer of cleansing and refilling. This is a time to ask questions of the supervisor. It is a great time for continued learning.

Glossary of Integrated Terms

Because we are working from Judeo-Christian paradigm some of the terms within this manual will most likely be unfamiliar with those not familiar with this particular religious culture. Therefore this glossary of integrated terms is an endeavor to provide a basis for understanding some of the terms strategic to the concepts present in this manual.

Believer - one who has a vital life connection with God through Jesus Christ

Bondages - Fortress or stronghold. State of superimposed influence on the soul (mind, will and emotions) thoughts, feelings, and decisions.

Circumcision of the Heart - a metaphorical term used throughout the Bible speaking of a "cutting away" of an area of the heart that is not life giving and productive.

Confess - from two Greek words meaning literally, "to speak the same as God" – so the idea is that you speak what God says about whatever you are "confessing"

Curse - outward expression of a critical, judgmental thought process

Demons - spirit emissaries of Satan; some theologians say that they are the other "fallen angels" that were deposed from heaven along with Lucifer (Satan).

Devil / Satan - personification of evil; in Judeo-Christian writings of antiquity Satan is depicted as the once "chief worship angel"

deposed from heaven due to pride & rebellion, thrown to earth by God, now seeking to oppose God by bringing harm to mankind whom are the object of God's love and affection.

False Identity - (Fig Leaves). A false identity is rooted to a false covering. The state or fact of being the same. The state or fact of being a specific person or thing. Source of significance, worth, and a sense of belonging.

Iniquity - desire, bent, propensity

Judgment - a process of evaluation which brings about a resolve concerning the ones judged. This word speaks of a process that begins with the collection of information (usually through the senses) and concludes with the resolve of right/wrong as well as the consequences for said actions.

Lies - A false statement (absent of truth) made with the intent to deceive.

Iniquity anchors to a lie and sustains the scheme.

Iniquity is based on desire.

A lie believed, removed faith. In the vacuum of faith, iniquity finds expression.

Lies, Three basic
1. God does not really love me.
2. Life is unfair.
3. I am not in His image...I am deformed in some way.

Lord = in reference to God

MP = Multiple Personality Disorder = **Dis-associative Identity Disorder** - Dissociation lies on a continuum ranging from the normal phenomena of day dreaming, fantasy, and "highway hypnosis" on the one end to the poly-fragmented (highly complex) multiple whose mind is split into hundreds (or thousands) of separate identities on the other end. This condition was formerly known as Multiple Personality Disorder (MPD), but was changed to Dis-associative Identity Disorder (DID) in 1994 by the American Psychiatric Association with its publication of DSM-IV, in order to more accurately describe the disorder.

Roots
- **Hereditary:** iniquity passed down.
- **Vow:** A solemn affirmation. To promise or declare. Usually an inward expression
- **Curse:** A violent expression of evil upon others. Usually an outward expression
- **Sin:** missing the mark. Can be in word, thought, or deed
- **Judgments:** Judging, deciding. An expression of opinion or estimate. Usually connected with a vow or a curse.
- **Wounds:** The results of a perceived need being met the wrong way. Keeps the root alive. Based on perception.

Sin = literally means, *to miss the mark*; destructive behavior which limits, reduces or withholds *life and it's innate qualities.*

Soul Tie = the soul is in reference to "the mind, the will and the emotions." A *Soul-Tie* occurs when a part of the mind, will and emotions (soul) is connected to something in the past (usually a relationship, a person, or emotion) through one of the senses. For example, is there a perfume that causes you to flash back to a particular relationship? Some call it nostalgia, or de ja vu.

Standards, False (Values) = That by which you judge. Standards are fixed boundaries. Values determine priority of importance. Something established as a rule of basis of comparison. In measuring quantity, quality, value, etc.

Strongs = in reference to a widely used & accepted *concordance* which gives English translations of both Greek and Hebrew words.

System / Schemes
- A plan, system or web of iniquities designed to ensnare people.
- A fleshly system that ensures the meeting of one's perceived needs.
- The enablement of the fig leaf.
- Originates in the mind and reigns in the heart.
- A network of iniquities designed to extract our anointing.

Transgression = decision or choice
Vow = inward determination resulting from a judgment

Counseling Aid Sheet

Explanation for water baptism:
1. Many times it seems impossible to break certain habits or patterns of behavior. There seems to be a hold within that is too difficult for the person to break. This is due to the hold that the flesh has on the soul.
2. This hold can be broken through death to the flesh. Such death comes about legally by water baptism. (Romans 6:3-6) It will have to be worked out experientially through faith and obedience.
3. Baptism circumcises the heart to cut away the hold of the flesh. (Colossians 2:10-13)
4. The believer should understand and claim this death to the flesh and circumcision of the heart at the time of baptism.
5. Be baptized in the name of Jesus.
6. Receive the benefits of baptism by faith.

Ministering to sin problems:

Getting rid of sin is a matter of confession and repentance. However, different roots of bondage and sin need different approaches in ministry in addition to confession and repentance.

For all sin:
> The person needs to confess the sin, repent, and receive forgiveness.

Transgression:
> May require deliverance. Confess as sin, repent, and receive forgiveness.
>
> Iniquity:
> 1. Cut soul ties at both ends, from ancestor and from person
> 2. Renounce all ground the enemy has taken through iniquity. Take back the ground.
> 3. Administer water baptism to circumcise the heart.
> 4. Call for the baptism of fire. Ask for the spirit of judging to judge the iniquity and the spirit of burning to burn out iniquity.
> 5. Replace the iniquity with the positive.

Steps to break trans-generational iniquity:
> 1. The person must confess the sins of the ancestors in the area of the iniquity.
> 2. He must confess his own sin and his own iniquity, or bent, toward that sin. Repent.
> 3. Then pray over that iniquity, break the power of the sin.
> 4. Break the soul ties between that person and each ancestor that is connected or involved. Break the tie of the ancestor to the bondage, break the tie connecting to the bondage with the person to whom we are ministering, and break the connection between the ancestor and the person to whom we are ministering. The person needs to confess that he renounces the birthright of that ancestor. **"I renounce the birthright of my grandmother to me. I renounce iniquity that has passed from her to me. I break every tie and lineage connected between us."**
> 5. Break every assignment of the enemy against that family. Cut them off from following that family line by the blood of Jesus.
> 6. Water baptism is also important.

Steps for breaking verbal curses:
1. Be in covenant with Jesus. Confess sin, repent, receive forgiveness.
2. Verbally break the curse and get released. "In the name of Jesus. I break the power of the curse of_____. I command that curse to fall to the ground and have no more effect in my life. Spirit of _____, I command you to release me in the name of Jesus."
3. Renounce all the ground the enemy has gained through that curse. "Devil, I have confessed as sin receiving and acting upon the curse of _____. It is no longer a part of my life. I put it under the blood of Jesus. Now I take back any ground that I have given you in my life through that curse in the name of Jesus."
4. Replace the sin with a blessing. "Lord Jesus, I trust in your word on_____. I receive that blessing for my life." (Replace the curse with the answer to that sin from the word. Example: replace bitterness with forgiveness, etc. Speak this to your soul.)
5. Meditate on the word in that area. Allow it to bring strength and healing.

Breaking Judgments:
1. Confess all bitterness and unforgiveness as sin. Repent and receive forgiveness.
2. Confess the judgment as sin. Repent and receive forgiveness.
3. Confess as sin taking the place of God as the only right judge. Repent and receive forgiveness.
4. Forgive and release people you have judged. That means to release them from your expectations. Your hope is in the Lord, not in them.
5. Tear down the false standards by which you judged.
6. Address the enemy and take back any ground given to him because of the above sins.
7. Break the sowing and reaping principle. Declare that because of repentance, you will not reap what you have sown. Ask for God's mercy and grace.

8. Pray concerning any restitution that the Lord would have you make in the situation, such as asking the person's forgiveness for having judged Him.
9. Pray blessings upon the person.

Breaking Vows:
1. Recognition. Ask the Holy Spirit to reveal to you any vows that you made. Ask Him to bring to your memory any such situations or any such determinations that you may have made in your heart.
2. Repent for any sinful reactions which caused you to make the vow - hate, resentment, vengeance, judgment, bitterness, fear, shame, etc.
3. Confess as sin taking that area of your life out of God's control by making a vow. Repent and receive forgiveness.
4. Take the authority of the name of Jesus and renounce the vow. Take back the ground that it gave the devil in your life.
5. Renounce the vow. Give that area of your life to the lordship of Jesus. Put it under His blood and declare Him to be Lord to do His will.
6. Set your heart upon the Lord. (Psalms 57:7; Psalms 112:7,8)
7. Persevere. Place the word which puts God's control in the area where the vow was in your heart. Stand firm in what the word says and in keeping your heart fixed on God.
8. Be water baptized, asking the Lord to circumcise your heart and cut away all effects of every wrong vow.

Christ-O-Therapy

1. **Observe the behavior** – key to changing behavior is discipline unto the fruit of the Holy Spirit. The process of change involves imitation and discipline until the behavior is voluntary.
2. **Discover the Roots** – using a history profile inventory, you can search for various patterns of behavior. These patterns of behavior will disclose possible roots. Critical relationships, i.e. father, mother, spouse, etc., will also need to be inventoried to discover

possible roots. Each root has a specific "cause and effect" therefore, each root must be dealt with individually.
3. **Discover the Lie** – behind each root there is a general lie that operates. After discovering the lie, replace it with truth. A process of "renewing the mind" is necessary for a complete paradigm change, especially as it pertains to changing from the False Identity to a Legitimate Identity.
4. **Diagram the Behavior System (scheme).** Using the "Schemes Chart" outline the Behavior System.
   - Take away legal ground through renunciation, confession, sin line and breaking judgments as appropriate.
   - Dismantle Schemes - Take place of death - (circumcision/baptism)
   - Bring totally to light through confession
   - Set accountability
   - Remove or separate destructive relationships
   - Provide healthy boundaries
5. **False Identity (Fig Leaf)** - Expose the False Identity.
   - Confess lie which produces the wrong identity
   - Confess right identity in place
6. **Outline the Values and Standards** that support the False Identity. Interrupt and replace the values & standards.
7. **Dysfunction** – "*Christo - Therapy*" is needed to complete the Restoration process. Besides the already mentioned facets of the Restoration process, some additional aids might include:
   - Accountability – personal accountability may be needed to reinforce the weakened behavior
   - Support Groups – helpful in aiding one in "processing" problems
   - Personal Discipleship – necessary for ongoing growth and personal development.
8. **Healing of heart / Memories / Child within** – this part of "Christo-Therapy" may involve a type of "prophetic counseling" where "words of knowledge" and "words of wisdom" are instrumental. Remember, *Wounds* keep roots alive

Pre-Counseling Inventory

An honest inventory is the place to begin. Here are some questions to answer to aid you in your heart's restoration:
Describe who you are.

- How do you deal with stress & pressure? (workout, eat, movies, sports, read, etc)

- What is necessary in a relationship for you to trust the other person?

- How do you show love to others?

- Do you feel secure? _____ What comprises "security" for you?

- Who do you get affirmation from the most?_____
- Who do you desire affirmation from the most?_____
- Describe your relationship to your father, listing the three most significant moments with him that have affected your life.

1.

2.

3.

- Describe your relationship to your mother, listing the three most significant moments with her that have affected your life.
1.

2.

3.

Issues

- What is the worst offence you have experienced? How did you handle it?

- What makes you angry?

- How do you handle the situation when you get angry?

- When do you get most embarrassed? Describe the circumstances.

- When do you have the most trouble making decisions? Describe the circumstances.

- Describe the circumstances that cause you to feel the most rejected.

- When do you feel most content? What comprises this feeling of contentment?

- Describe your greatest fear.

- Describe how you began your relationship with God, and what is essential to you to continue this relationship.

- Describe any experiences you have had with séances, fortune tellers, psychics, drugs, other occult practices.

- Please list all medications you presently take.

Issues

Counseling Ledger

Name_____Phone ( )_____

Church_____Pastor _____

Church Phone ( ) _____email _____

Notes:
(/ /) –

Next Appt: (/ /)

Notes:
(/ /) –

Next Appt: (/ /)

Notes:
(/ /) –

Next Appt: (/ /)

Notes:
(/ /) –

Next Appt: (/ /)

Issues

Child Information Form

IDENTIFYING INFORMATION
Child's Name_____Nickname_____
Date of Birth_____ Sex: M F   Present Age _____
School Attending _____Grade _____ Teacher _____
Birth Order: 1st 2nd 3rd 4th 5th 6th of 1 2 3 4 5 6 children
Child lives with _____
Name of Parents/Guardians _____
Address _____
Home Phone _____Work Phone(s) _____

MAJOR CONCERNS
Please describe, in your own words, your concerns about your child and the reasons that you are seeking help:_____
_____
_____
_____

When were these difficulties first noticed? Please explain as fully as you can._____
_____
_____

Has this child had any previous counseling or other professional assistance with the problems stated here? If so, please provide information:

 Counselor/professional   Approximate dates   What was done?
_____
_____
_____
_____

MEDICAL HISTORY
Please describe this child's general health._____
_____
_____

Has he/she had any serious illnesses, accidents, or injuries?_____
_____
_____

Please give reason and approximate dates for any hospitalizations.__

Are there any conditions that require regular medical care_____

Does this child take any medications on a regular basis? If so, please note type of medication and frequency of use._____

Does the child have any difficulties with vision or hearing? Note date and results of any previous vision or hearing examinations._____

Does the child have any allergies? If yes, please identify._____

Name of pediatrician/family physician_____
Date of last physical examination_____

DEVELOPMENTAL HISTORY

Please note any complications during pregnancy with this child (such as illness, accidents, prolonged emotional stress, etc.)_____

Delivery was: on time _____ early _____ late _____
Length of labor_____
Any complications?_____
Birth weight _____ Incubator? _____Need oxygen? _____
How would you describe your child as an infant?_____

Issues

Has this child had any problems with motor development (such as difficulty learning to walk; poor coordination; difficulty coloring, cutting, or drawing)? _____
_____

At what age was the child able to:
Smile and recognize people _____ Feed self with spoon_____
Sit up without support _____ Drink from glass/cup_____
Stand alone _____ Ride a tricycle_____
Walk alone _____ Tie shoes_____
Has this child had any problems with understand or speaking language?_____
_____

At what age (month/years and months) was this child able to:
Coo and babble _____ Combine two words_____
Say first words _____ Follow simple directions_____
Name people and things _____ Use short sentences_____
Does this child have current problems with soiling or wetting during the day or at night?_____
If so, explain_____
_____

At what age did this child:
Begin toilet training _____ Complete toilet training_____
Remain dry during the day _____ Remain dry during the night___
Does this child have current sleep disturbances, such as difficulty falling asleep, getting up in the middle of the night, or being difficult to wake?_____
_____
_____

LEARNING DEVELOPMENT

Compared to other children you know, this child did/does have difficulty with

	Did	Does
Identifying basic colors	___	___
Learning the alphabet	___	___
Learning to count	___	___
Recognizing numbers	___	___
Reading	___	___
Printing	___	___
Spelling correctly	___	___
Comprehension of reading	___	___
Telling time	___	___
Adding numbers	___	___
Subtracting	___	___
Multiplying	___	___
Dividing	___	___
Cursivewriting	___	___

Please note 5the grades and explain the circumstances if this child has:
_____
(1) Had extended or frequent absences_____
(2) Had to repeat the year_____
(3) Changed schools in mid-year_____
(4) Began school year at a new school_____
Briefly describe how this child is doing in school. Note current marks and areas of strength or weakness in school work._____
_____
Has he/she had any remedial help or special education services in school or privately?_____
_____
Please describe this child's attitude toward school. Note any special interests or dislikes he/she has in school._____
_____
How does this child get along with the teacher and other students in school?_____

Issues

_____
_____

SOCIAL DEVELOPMENT AND PEER RELATIONSHIPS

What special interests, hobbies, sports, and games does the child enjoy both in and after school?_____
_____

When this child chooses playmates, are they:
Older   younger   own age   all ages boys
Girls   both boys & girls

In play activities, is the child a leader, or a follower, or a loner?_____

Does the child prefer the company of adults to other children?
Yes   No

Does this child have at least one best friend?
Yes   No

What is the friends age & name? _____

EMOTIONAL DEVELOPMENT

Has your child ever been characterized by family members, teachers or others as being:

	Yes	No		Yes	No
Restless/inattentive	___	___	Forgetful	___	___
Humorous/fun	___	___	Quick to Anger	___	___
Cheerful	___	___	Depressed/sad	___	___
Daydreamer	___	___	Disruptive	___	___
Immature	___	___	Happy	___	___
Aggressive	___	___	Nervous/tense	___	___

Does this child have a great many fears or worries? If so, what are they?_____
_____

Does this child have unusual or persistent nightmares? If so, what are they about?_____
_____

SPECIAL CONCERNS

Briefly describe this child's behavior at home_____

Issues

Please check below any past or present concerns; then give the age during which they occurred.

Speech _____	Destructiveness _____
Eating _____	Physical health _____
Sleeping _____	Fears _____
Activity level _____	Bladder control _____
Coordination _____	Bowel function _____
Aggressive _____	Temper tantrums _____
Sexual activity _____	Lying _____
Stealing _____	Fire setting _____
Sucking thumb _____	Anxiety _____
Responsible _____	Other _____

Please elaborate on any concerns that you have about any of the difficulties listed. _____

Describe special strengths the child has shown in his/her overall adjustment to past difficulties _____

FAMILY REALTIONSHIPS

Have any of the following potential problems been present in the child's family? If so, state which of the family members experienced the problem (M-mother, F-father, B-brother, S-sister, GM-grandmother, etc.)

Career overworking _____	Multiple moves _____
Physical health _____	Financial pressures _____
Mental health _____	Marital problems _____
Death of family member _____	Separation _____
Drinking _____	Divorce _____
Sibling rivalry _____	Abandonment _____

OTHER

If you were to describe your child as a person and not as a son or daughter, what would you say about him or her? _____

SIGNATURE(S) OF PARENT OR PARENTS WHO COMPLETED THIS FORM

Father _____ Date _____
Mother _____ Date _____
Guardian _____ Date _____

RELEASE OF LIABILITY

For Christ-O-Therapy Counseling

FOR AND IN CONSIDERATION OF Dr. Bob Nichols and Foundations II Ministries, Inc; provision of ministerial and counseling services, the undersigned, being legally competent and fully authorized and empowered to do so, does hereby RELEASE, ACQUIT, AND FOREVER DISCHARGE Dr. Bob Nichols and Foundations II Ministries, Inc., and all participating ministers, counselors and therapists connected to said ministry, from any and all actions, courses of action, claims, demands, damages, costs, loss of service, expenses and compensation, on account of any and all known and unknown personal injuries, mental anguish or agitation, and damage claims to person or property resulting from or arising out of or related to ministerial services and/or counseling ministry provided by Dr. Bob Nichols and Foundations II Ministries, Inc., and/or agents, representatives and/or employees in any way affecting the undersigned parties.

By law, there are certain situations in which information about individuals undergoing such ministry may be released with or without their permission. These situations are as follows:

1. Where children are currently being physically abused, neglected, or sexually abused, the proper authorities must be notified.
2. In emergency situations where there may be danger to the client or others as with homicide or suicide, confidentiality may be broken.

The undersigned parties fully understand that the ministerial services to be provided are Distinctively Christian in nature, and freely enter into such ministerial services with full knowledge of the nature of the services they are about to receive.

The undersigned parties further state that they are accepting the preceding of their own free will and accord, and have not been unduly influenced or persuaded by anyone to participate in this counseling ministry. The undersigned parties state that they are seeking ministry from Dr. Bob Nichols and Foundations II Ministries, Inc., of their own free will, and fully understand that all counseling ministry is advisory in nature and that decisions and actions taken by said undersigned parties based on anything said by Dr. Nichols or any representative, employ or associate of Foundations II Ministries, are ultimately their own decisions and actions, and that said undersigned parties take full responsibility for their decisions and actions.

The undersigned further AGREE to indemnify, have and hold harmless Dr. Bob Nichols, Foundations II Ministries, Inc., it's Board of Directors, it's agents, including any residences, any offices or any churches where counseling ministry may take place, and any employees from any and all claims and damages of every kind to person or property arising out of or attributed to the spiritual, psychological, and/or mental problems which brought the undersigned to Dr. Bob Nichols, Foundations II Ministries, Inc., or to the undersigned at any point after the date of this release.

IT IS FURTHER UNDERSTOOD AND AGREED that this waiver and release constitutes an admission and acknowledgment by this undersigned that they have received no warranty, guarantee, or promise of any particular result either expressed or implied, from

Dr. Bob Nichols, Foundations II Ministries, Inc., it's agents, representatives, employees, or Board of Directors. The undersigned parties acknowledge and agree that the very nature of their problems (s) is necessarily such that no specific result (s) can be promised or warranted by any such ministry.

This release contains the entire agreement between the parties hereto, and the terms of this waiver and release are contractual and not mere recital. The undersigned further states they have carefully read the foregoing release, know the contents thereof, and sign the same of their own free act and deed.

Signed:_____ Date: _____
Signature of Client indicating informed consent and acceptance of above.

PLEASE PRINT CLEARLY

Name _____

Address _____

City _____

Province/State_____

Postal/Zip Code _____

Phone _____Cell _____

Email_____

Signature of Witness _____

Printed Name & Address of Witness: _____

_____

_____

MINOR RELEASE (LEGAL PARENT(s) / LEGAL GUARDIAN(s) PLEASE SIGN)
Signed: _____ Date: _____
Signature of Parent/Guardian indicating informed consent and acceptance of above.
Date _____
Minor client, 12-17 years inclusive _____
Date _____

Witness _____

Date _____

INFORMED CONSENT FOR PARTICIPATING IN COUNSELING OR "CHRIST-O-THERAPY" WITH DR. BOB NICHOLS OR A COUNSELOR OF FOUNDATIONS II MINISTRIES, INC.

DIAGNOSIS/ASSESSMENT AND REASONS FOR USING "CHRIST-O-THERAPY": It is important for you to understand that Dr. Bob Nichols, Foundations II Ministries, Inc., (hereinafter known as Counselor) diagnosis/assessment regarding your symptoms/problems, and for you to understand why the Counselor may think CHRIST-O-THERAPY will be helpful. The best way for us to accomplish this is to discuss these two issues prior to your first session.

WHAT TO EXPECT: It is important for you to know the basic details of what to expect as you participate in the counseling sessions.
- Client fills out a *Pre-counseling Inventory, Confidentiality Agreement, release of liability* forms prior to the first session
- A counseling team (2 people) will meet you at a predetermined location comfortable to both counselors and client.
- Session one is a time for the client to share their perspective and story about their present situation.
- Other diagnostic questions will be asked as the counselor sees need.
- A plan-of-therapy will be outlined and followed for the successive sessions.

DIFFERENCES IN INDIVIDUAL EXPERIENCE AND TIME FRAMES: It is important to realize that there is a wide range of experiences with counseling. Some receive healing very quickly, and are free of their presenting symptoms in one or two sessions. For others the process goes much more slowly. Sometimes, even when the process is working correctly, the presenting symptoms can still be present after many months of hard work. The time frames are also dependent on the number and severity of lie-based memories that are currently impacting your life.

NO GUARANTEE: It is also important to realize that there is no way to guarantee results with any form of psychotherapy or counseling, including Christ-O-Therapy. Some people receive important healing with Christ-O-Therapy, and others may not be able to use Christ-O-Therapy (for reasons we sometimes do not understand).

OPTIONS OTHER THAN CHRIST-O-THERAPY: Our counselor uses Christ-O-Therapy in much of the work that counselor does because our counselor believes it to be an effective and cost and time efficient tool. However, it is important that you realize there are other options. If you do not wish to participate in Christ-O-Therapy, and would rather use other healing tools, such as cognitive therapy, behavioral therapy, relaxation techniques, psychiatric medications, or other forms of prayer for emotional healing, this is your choice. It is also important for you to be aware of the option to use psychiatric medication (s) and/or nutrient solutions in combination with Christ-O-Therapy.

RISKS AND BENEFITS OF CHRIST-O-THEREAPY AND OF OTHER OPTIONS: In any form of therapy and/or counseling that includes working with traumatic memories; there is a real risk that "things will feel worse before they feel better." You may experience intense negative emotions, and even painful physical sensations, as a part of going through traumatic memories. Christ-O-Therapy may uncover unresolved issues, traumatic memories, and painful emotions that you have not anticipated. Sometimes the issues and/or memories brought forward during a session cannot be fully resolved by the end of the session. You may continue to process painful material between counseling sessions, and this processing between sessions may include uncovering additional painful material.

One often unanticipated "risk" is that you will change. If you receive significant healing, you will change, and this will affect many aspects of your life (for example, your satisfaction with your current career and how you relate to your family and friends). The biggest benefit - the biggest reason to use a treatment option that involves the risks of working with traumatic memories - is that these treatment options resolve the roots of the problem and thereby accomplish permanent healing. These risks and benefits pertain to any form of therapy or ministry that involves working with traumatic memories, including Christ-O-Therapy, all other forms of prayer for emotional healing that I am aware of, as well as cognitive-behavioral therapy.

REGARDING COMPARATIVE RISKS AND BENEFITS: Our counselor personal assessment is that, for most people, Christ-O-Therapy works more quickly and with less risk of symptom exacerbation than any other therapy or ministry that includes working with traumatic memories. Forms of treatment that focus primarily on symptom control, and that do not include working with old traumatic memories, include very little risk of temporarily increasing symptoms by "uncovering" painful memories and emotions. Relaxation techniques, some forms of cognitive therapy, and many psychiatric medications are examples of "symptom control" treatment options. Each psychiatric medication has its own risks and side effects, but the biggest risk of these symptom control treatment options is that they are temporary solutions and do not address the underlying issues. If they are not used in combination with a therapy or counseling that resolves the underlying roots, then various symptoms/problems will keep coming back, often at very inconvenient times and places. Another risk of "symptom control" treatment options is that they can make it more difficult to find and resolve the underlying roots of the symptoms.

CONSENT TO PARTICIPATE IN CHRIST-O-THERAPY: Our relationship is confidential, protected by the ethics of the American Psychological Association and statutes of Texas. There are, however, three exceptions when I have a moral and legal duty to inform others: when you (1) discuss your intent to harm someone; (2) inform me you consider hurting yourself; and (3) describe a future illicit act. While your interests and welfare are my primary concerns, when believing you want to hurt yourself or others, I will intervene.

Please sign signifying you understand the three provisions stated herein. If you cannot agree to this arrangement, then it makes sense for you to work with someone else. If you violate this contact by not discussing your behavior with me before you act, I reserve the right to terminate our relationship.

Signed:_____ Date: _____
Signature of Client indicating informed consent and acceptance of above.

PLEASE PRINT CLEARLY (printed client name and witness name and witness signature ONLY are required if the same as the above)

Name _____

Address _____

City _____

Province/State_____

Postal/Zip Code _____

Phone _____Cell _____

Email_____

Signature of Witness _____

Printed Name & Address of Witness: _____

_____

MINOR RELEASE (LEGAL PARENT(s) / LEGAL GUARDIAN(s) PLEASE SIGN)

_____
Signature of Parent/Guardian indicating informed consent and acceptance of above.

Issues

Date _____

Minor client, 12-17 years inclusive _____

Witness _____

Printed in the United States
200845BV00001B/133-1023/A